DOWN SYNDROME
issues and information

Overview

An overview of the development of teenagers with Down syndrome (11-16 years)

Sue Buckley and Ben Sacks

Summary - Research studies demonstrate that young people with Down syndrome make significant progress in all areas of their development during their teenage years and into early adult life. For all young people, adolescence is a period of development which is characterised by a shift from dependence to independence. At 11 years, most young people are still largely supervised in the community and supported by parents in all aspects of their lives. By 18 years, most young people are quite independent in travelling, managing money, choosing friends and leisure interests, taking care of their personal daily needs and will be on the way to leaving the family home. This life period is also important for deciding on future occupation, life style and personal identity. It is also a period of significant physical, sexual and emotional development, when establishing close friendships, dating and partners become important. In this module it is argued that the physical, social and emotional needs of teenagers with Down syndrome are essentially the same as those of other teenagers and should be recognised as such. The priority for parents and teachers should be to support them through these changes with the goal of encouraging as much independence and personal control over their lives as possible. This is also important for developing their self esteem, personal identities and adjustment to the understanding of what having Down syndrome means for their adult lives. In addition, it is argued that teenagers with Down syndrome can continue to develop their basic skills in speech, language, literacy and numeracy and that teaching for these should continue through adolescence with age-appropriate adaptations to the content of teaching programmes.

Series Editors

Sue Buckley and Gillian Bird

DSii-01-06-(en-gb) (February, 2002)

http://www.down-syndrome.net/library/dsii/01/06/

First published: February, 2002

ISBN: 1-903806-03-8

A publication of The Down Syndrome Educational Trust

The Sarah Duffen Centre, Belmont Street, Southsea,
Hampshire, PO5 1NA, United Kingdom.

Telephone	+44 (0)23 9285 5330
Facsimile	+44 (0)23 9285 5320
E-mail	enquiries@downsed.org
Web Site	http://www.downsed.org/

The Down Syndrome Educational Trust is a charity, registered in England and Wales (number 1062823).

Proceeds from this publication support future research, services and publications.

The right of Sue Buckley and Ben Sacks to be identified as authors of this Work has been asserted by them in accordance with sections 77 and 78 of the Copyright, Designs and Patents Act 1988.

Copyright © The Down Syndrome Educational Trust 2002. All Rights Reserved.

No part of this publication may be reproduced, or transmitted, in any form or by any means, or stored in a retrieval system of any nature, without the prior written permission of the publisher. Any person who does any unauthorised act in relation to this publication may be liable to criminal prosecution and civil claims for damages.

This book is sold subject to the condition that it shall not, by way of trade or otherwise, be lent, re-sold, hired out or otherwise circulated without the publisher's prior consent in any form of binding or cover other than that in which it is published and without a similar condition including this condition being imposed on the subsequent publisher.

Concept and design: Frank Buckley and Linda Hall

Typeset, printed and distributed by a wholly-owned subsidiary of The Down Syndrome Educational Trust:

DownsEd Limited
The Sarah Duffen Centre, Belmont Street,
Southsea, Hampshire, PO5 1NA.
United Kingdom.

Contents

Introduction 1

I. Development during teenage years 3
What do typically developing teenagers achieve? 3
What goals should we set for teenagers with Down syndrome? 4
Major trends in development 7
In summary 15
What levels of achievement can we expect? 16
Personal care and daily living skills 16
Motor skills 18
Speech and Language 18
Reading and writing 19
Number, money and time 20
Social and interpersonal development 21
Achievements at 16 years 23
Individual differences 24

Meeting the educational and developmental needs of teenagers with Down syndrome 26
Health and sensory impairments 27
A specific developmental profile 27
Education 29
Meeting the specific educational needs associated with Down syndrome in special or mainstream classes 31
Goals for teachers of 11-16 year olds with Down syndrome 31
Speech and language therapy 31
Goals for speech and language therapists working with 11-16 year olds with Down syndrome 32
Motor skills 33
Goals for occupational therapists and physiotherapists 33

Family issues 33
Goals for parents of 11-16 year olds with Down syndrome 34

In summary 34

II. Health care for teenagers with Down syndrome 35
Hearing disorders 36
Disorders of vision 40
Disorders of thyroid function 41
Infection in people with Down syndrome 43
Gastro-intestinal system 43
Cardio-vascular system 44

    Atlanto-axial instability 44
    Sleep Related Breathing Problems 46
    Obesity, healthy eating and exercise 47
    Dental care.. 48
    Puberty and sexual health 48
    Mental Health and Behaviour Problems... 49

Monitoring developmental progress 51
References 52

Authors

Sue Buckley
Emeritus Professor of Developmental Disability, Psychology Department, University of Portsmouth, UK
Director of Research and Training, The Down Syndrome Educational Trust, UK.

Ben Sacks
Consultant Developmental Psychiatrist and Medical Advisor to The Down Syndrome Educational Trust, UK. Formerly Professor of Developmental Psychiatry, Charing Cross and Westminster Medical Schools, The University of London, London, UK.

Acknowledgements

The authors would like to thank all the children, teenagers and adults with Down syndrome, and the families and practitioners that they have been privileged to work with over many years. We hope that all we have learned from them is reflected in our writing. However, the opinions expressed and any errors remain the sole responsibility of the authors.

Terminology

The term 'learning difficulty' is used throughout this module as it is the term currently in common use in the United Kingdom. The terms 'mental retardation', 'intellectual impairment', and 'developmental disability' are equivalent terms, used in other parts of the world.

The term 'teenagers' has been used as the generic term for this age group, even though the youngest are 11 year olds, as 'children' is no longer appropriate.

An overview of the development of teenagers with Down syndrome (11-16 years)

Introduction

The aim of this module is to provide an overview of development during the period from eleven to sixteen years and to assist the reader in integrating the material covered in the other DSii modules for this age group. These modules each cover specific aspects of development, i.e. motor, social and behavioural, speech and language, working memory, reading and numeracy, and family issues, in detail. The years 11 to 16 were chosen as these are the secondary school years in the UK system, with teenagers usually moving to further education colleges at 17 years. However, much of the information in these modules will be relevant to early adulthood (18-20 years).

This module is intended to help parents, families, teachers, speech and language therapists, and other practitioners who work with young people in this age range. In the authors' experience, they all wish to know *what developmental and educational progress to expect for a teenager with Down syndrome* and *how to help the teenager to progress as fast as possible*.

These two main questions are addressed, within the context of the wide range of individual differences in rates of development of young people with Down syndrome. In order to answer the question of how to help teenagers to progress, the reasons for their particular developmental profile are outlined as far as they are known, as this information should help to identify effective therapy and teaching strategies. The question of how to help also leads to a discussion of the importance of balancing family needs with the needs of the teenager with Down syndrome.

In the authors' view, in order to understand the ways in which having Down syndrome affects teenagers' development it is necessary to consider what is known about the development of typically developing young people. In the last thirty years, there have been considerable advances in our understanding of the processes of development, particularly in the areas of social learning, cognition and language. The greater our understanding of typical development, the easier it is to begin to understand the effects of a disabling condition such as Down syndrome on the processes of development. As we identify the specific effects of Down syndrome on development, we are in a better position to develop effective interventions and teaching strategies.

This is the approach taken throughout the DSii modules. We draw on research into the development of typically developing young people, the specific research into the development of young people with Down syndrome and research that has evaluated effective interventions and teaching strategies, where they exist.

To date, there is not a great deal of research into the development of teenagers with Down syndrome or the issues which affect their progress. The authors have drawn on their own studies with teenagers and their parents in Hampshire to inform these modules,[1,2,3] and included the information from any other relevant published studies wherever possible.

Age-appropriate goals

In addition to using this information to understand the young people's developmental and learning difficulties, we assess the major developmental achievements of typically developing young people over the age span and consider the relevance of these for setting targets for teenagers with Down syndrome.

Teenagers with Down syndrome are *people first*, with the same rights to be full citizens in the adult community in a few years time, and the same needs. The reader is reminded that this view is expressed eloquently by a number of young adults with Down syndrome in the *Living with Down syndrome* module in this series.[Dsii-01-01] If individuals with Down syndrome are to be fully included in the community, as teenagers and as adults, it is important to recognise that their place in society will be linked to their chronological age, and that this is right and appropriate.

As teenagers, young people with Down syndrome reach puberty at about the same age as other young people. As teenagers they develop typical leisure interests and awareness of sexuality.[1,2,3] The point being stressed is that we believe that it is important to recognise that the social and emotional needs of teenagers and adults are age-appropriate. Their status in the community and their role in life is mainly determined by their chronological age. Moving through school to college, work and independent living will happen on the basis of their chronological age.

Therefore the goals for education and social development need to be considered within this framework, and take account of the teenager's place in society. In the next section, the developmental achievements for typically developing teenagers are discussed to provide a baseline for setting targets for teenagers with Down syndrome across this life stage.

A time of significant progress

Many young people with Down syndrome make significant progress during their teenage years, as they begin to take more responsibility, become more independent and apply learning to activities that they can see as meaningful in their everyday lives.

The reasons for having age-appropriate expectations for teenagers with Down syndrome

- Teenagers with Down syndrome are *people first*, and wish to lead full lives, like anyone else
- Inclusion in schools and clubs is with same age peers, therefore expectations for social skills and behaviour need to be age-appropriate
- Leisure interests, emotional and social needs tend to be age-appropriate
- Moving through life - secondary school, puberty, further education, work, partners, leaving home - tends to be on the basis of age
- The challenge for parents and teachers is to treat the teenager in an age-appropriate manner, to respect their age, encourage confidence, independence and self-esteem, and facilitate their inclusion in the community
- The challenge for the teenager with Down syndrome, who may have limited speech, language and cognitive skills for his or her age, is to participate in life in an age-appropriate way

An overview of the development of teenagers with Down syndrome

Age:-	11	12	13	14	15	16	17	18	19	20

CHILD   **ADULT**

Dependence on family   **Independence**

- Practical — personal care, meals, homecare, clothes →
- Social — community, roads, buses, money, shopping →
- Emotional — form own relationships, friends, partners →
- Financial — pocket money — wages — own money →

Family home ——————————————————————— **Own home**
School ————————————————————————————— **Work**
Supervised leisure ——————————————————— **Own leisure**
Supervised friends ——————————————————— **Own friends**

        puberty ——————— sexuality ——————— partner
        self-awareness → who am I? → adult
        self-esteem ——— place in society? ——— identity

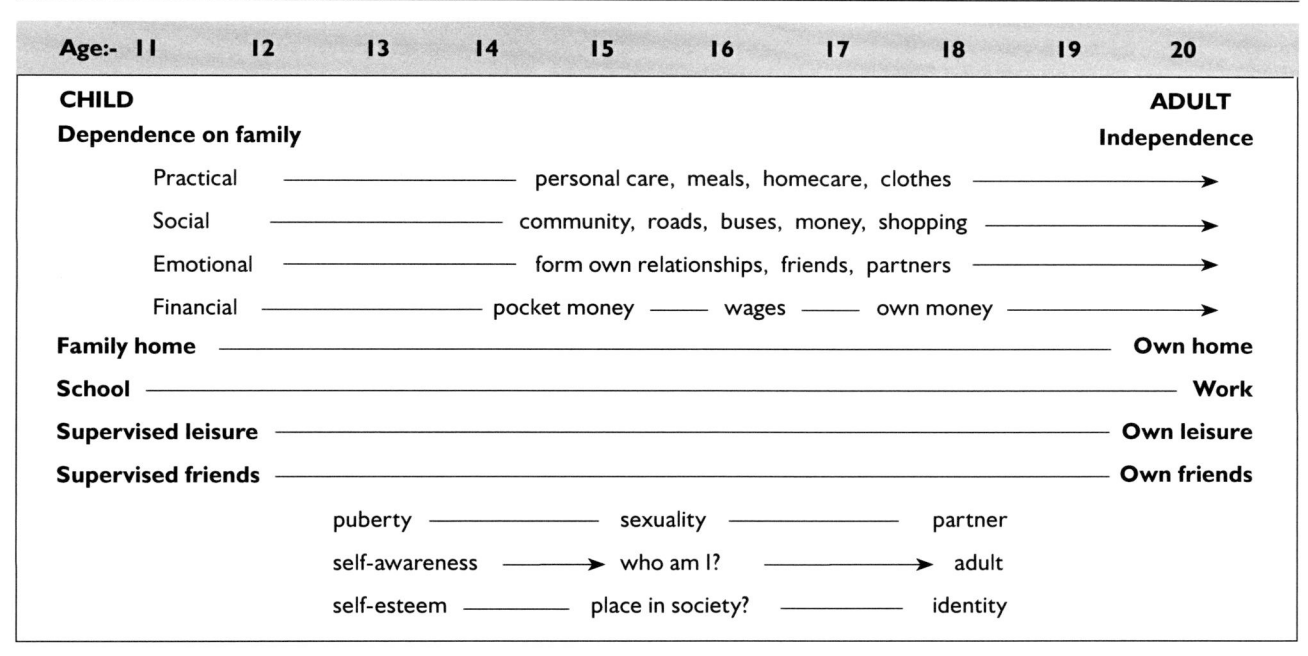

Figure 1. An overview of developmental progress during adolescence

1. Development during teenage years

What do typically developing teenagers achieve?

Independence from the family

It is possible to characterise the main developmental changes during teenage years as progress from dependence to independence and we have attempted to illustrate this in Figure 1. Most typically developing 11 year olds still need a high degree of support for all aspects of their daily lives, including personal daily care activities such as bathing, care of clothes, cleaning rooms and preparation of meals, travel and choice of social activities outside the home, and responsibility for money. By the end of the teenage period, most young people will be largely independent of their families. Many will be at work and others will be studying away from home; some will have their own homes. Almost everyone will be able to take care of all their personal daily care needs, laundry, shopping and cooking. Many will be living in their own home, some with partners by this age. Most will be managing their own money. Some will be driving and have a car of their own. This level of competence and independence also implies that most young people are able to behave in a socially appropriate and law-abiding manner, managing their emotions and behaviour appropriately in public, coping with the inevitable temptations of alcohol, smoking and drugs and are able to make and sustain friendships and relationships. In summary most young people are largely independent of their families by the time they reach 20 years of age even though emotional ties, social and financial support and advice from families will still be important.

A personal identity, friends and relationships

The teenage years are also a very important life period for establishing one's own personal identity. Teenagers discover their skills and aptitudes and make choices about future work and adult roles in society. They discover their personal values, styles of dress and preferred lifestyles, their choices of music,

An overview of the development of teenagers with Down syndrome

art and leisure activities. Teenagers also experience rapid growth and changes in body and facial appearance - attractiveness can become a big issue. They experience new emotions, puberty, sexuality and find special friends and sexual partners. All these aspects of teenage experience contribute to an individual's identity - how they see themselves - and to their self-confidence and self-esteem. Friends are a very important part of the teenage years, providing support and understanding through this often difficult time as teenagers become increasing self aware and experience self doubts. Adult role models for occupations and for lifestyles also play an important part in the teenager's development.

Cognitive and academic progress, preparations for work

Most teenagers make significant academic progress during their teenage years. All teenagers continue their education for some years - compulsory education continues to 16 years in the UK. Many continue their education and training in colleges or universities into their early adult lives. In the UK education to 19 years is supported for all young people in schools and further education colleges. After this age, many adult education and training opportunities are available through adult education colleges. During the teenage years, young people usually continue to develop their speech, language, literacy and numeracy skills and they expand their knowledge across many general curriculum subjects as well as subjects of their own particular choice. Young people increasingly specialise and choose to gain knowledge and skills in areas that they are interested in and for which they have an aptitude. The later years in education are usually a preparation for work roles in adult life.

What goals should we set for teenagers with Down syndrome?

In the authors' view, based on their experience of working with many teenagers and adults, and as parents, the goals for teenagers with Down syndrome should be essentially the same as those for typically developing teenagers i.e.:

- to become as independent as possible in their personal care and their social lives
- to develop a positive personal identity, self-confidence and self-esteem - to *feel good about themselves*
- to develop a network of friends, personal relationships and leisure interests
- to progress their cognitive, speech and language, and academic skills, and prepare for work

Independence and social competence

Parents and teachers need to encourage young people with Down syndrome to become as independent as possible in all areas of their lives. The young person's practical and social independence will increase their privacy and dignity as a person in teenage and adult years. It will also ensure that each individual develops all the skills that he or she is capable of and that each individual has a sense of control over their lives. Research has shown that any individual who feels helpless and who feels that he or she has no control over his or her life is vulnerable to depression and unhappiness. Those working with adults with Down syndrome have reported that the same factors affect the well-being and mental health of adults with Down syndrome.[4]

Social competence is an important part of being able to be independent. Social competence requires the ability to manage one's own behaviour and emotions in an age appropriate manner, the ability to interact appropriately with others in social situations such as in shops, restaurants or buses, and to make and sustain friendships.

Personal identity

All parents hope that their children will feel good about themselves - that they will develop a positive sense of who they are and their place in the world. This process may be more difficult for a teenager with Down syndrome and it is during their teenage years that young people with Down syndrome become more aware of the reality of their disability and the limits that this is going to place on their adult lives. It is not unusual for teenagers to show their distress as they see younger brothers and sisters going out alone, having boyfriends or girlfriends, learning to drive the car and then leaving home to start families of their own.

Many teenagers with Down syndrome do not have sufficient language ability to be able to express what they are feeling to family or friends and this can be a difficult time. In the authors' experience, some teenagers with Down syndrome may express their distress by becoming withdrawn or unco-operative, by having uncharacteristic outbursts off difficult or aggressive behaviour or by becoming clinically depressed. The majority of these young people come through this period and adjust to adult life but some will need professional support and treatment. Most teenagers with Down syndrome cope with adjusting to the pressures of adolescence without any outward signs of distress but this does not mean that the adjustment has not been painful for them at times.

Families need to be sensitive and not underestimate the young person's awareness of the issues because they cannot express them. It may help to have friends with Down syndrome or a similar level of learning disability. In times of stress, most of us find support in having friends who been through the same experiences and can empathise with what we are experiencing. It may also help if positive adult role models - adults with Down syndrome who are enjoying their lives - can be found in the teenager's own community. Videos are available, made by adults with Down syndrome with this need in mind, and they may prove helpful.[5,6] The reader may also find it useful to refer again to the views of adults with Down syndrome in the *Living with Down syndrome* module.[DSii-01-01] The degree to which a young person has some control over their lives and the choices they can make will also influence their adjustment. It is important to respect the right of the teenager to be treated in a chronologically appropriate way, and to try to avoid treating him/her as if he/she is younger.

Friends and social lives

Research into the mental health of all adults identifies the importance of networks for friendship and social support. Loneliness and social isolation increase vulnerability to misery and mental health problems. Friendships which provide mutual respect, understanding and emotional support become particularly important for young people during adolescence. Schools, social activities and clubs all provide the opportunity to make friends. However, teenagers with Down syndrome may be more dependent on the support of others to ensure that they actually go to leisure activities and clubs where they can make friends.

For teenagers in special education, it may be difficult to meet with school friends out of school as families may live too far from each other and the teenagers may not have independent travel skills. For teenagers in inclusive school settings, the friendships with non-disabled peers are different in that they are 'helping' friendships rather than mutually supportive, reciprocal friendships, and they may not continue out of school. The teenagers included in mainstream schools may not have enough opportunities to meet other teenagers with Down syndrome or a similar level of learning disability to establish friendships and parents may need to take active steps to create these opportunities out of school. Research discussed on pages 10 and 21 suggests that this is an issue which needs to be addressed.

Cognitive and academic progress

Research indicates that most teenagers with Down syndrome make significant progress in cognitive and academic skills and that the development of basic literacy and numeracy skills should be a priority during teenage years. Some teenagers will start their secondary education with significant reading and writing skills (at about an 8 year level) and some will have basic numeracy to a 6 to 7 year level, but many teenagers will start secondary school with minimal literacy and numeracy skills (5 to 6 year level) and develop these skills to a level of functional usefulness during their teenage years. Indeed, some observers suggest that many teenagers are ready to make progress because their general cognitive skills are sufficiently advanced and they are motivated to learn because they are now old enough to see the practical value of these skills in their daily lives.[7,8] They want to be able to read names, notices, messages and instructions and they want to understand and use money. For this reason, the modules on reading and number for 11-16 year olds in this series take a basic skills approach to teaching these skills and provide activities to take teenagers from the earliest stages to more advanced levels. There are no real short cuts to real understanding and competence in literacy or numeracy - the basic steps need to be understood before more advanced progress is possible - though there are short cuts to functional use which do not require full understanding and these are also included in the practical modules. However, parents and teachers are encouraged not to assume that teenagers will not understand the basics and therefore to opt for the functional approach too quickly, but to continue to give teenagers the opportunity to understand the basics.

Research also indicates that many teenagers make significant progress in speech and language during the teenage years so that this is also identified as a priority for parents, teachers and speech and language therapists. Many speech and language activities can be readily linked into the school curriculum and parents can also work on them during daily activities at home.

The whole range of targets that the authors believe to be priorities for teenagers with Down syndrome are summarised in Figure 2. The range of achievements which might be expected for each of these areas of development is summarised on pages 16-23. Before reviewing these expectations in detail, in

An overview of the development of teenagers with Down syndrome

Age:-	11 years	12 years	13 years	14 years	15 years	16 years	17 years
UK school year:	Year 7	Year 8	Year 9	Year 10	Year 11	F.E.	F.E.
Social/ interpersonal	games with friends, loose friendships		games with rules, joining clubs			increasing cooperation and teamwork special friends, boy/girlfriends, partners	
Self-help/ personal care	increasing personal independence — making snacks and meals, shopping, care of food — increasing independence in bathing/showering and choosing clothes, caring for nails and hair						
Motor skills	continuing to develop skill in drawing and handwriting — continuing to develop skills in physical education, ball control, sports						
Speech and language	talking in simple or telegraphic sentences improving communication improving intelligibility		learning more age-appropriate vocabulary and learning more grammar being able to share events, tell stories, initiate conversations, engage in social conversations speaking more clearly, being understood in the community			talking in sentences	
Reading and writing	continuing to develop reading and writing skills		recording of events and lessons		improving ability to spell		writing letters, cards, keeping a diary
Number	developing numeracy skills		continuing to improve counting and calculating skills (adding/subtracting tens and units)		developing time and money skills		applying number and money to daily activities
Working memory	digit span 2/3		increasing short-term spans				digit span 4/5
Behaviour	increasing maturity in school and at home		increasing responsibility for own behaviour age-appropriate, socially acceptable behaviour at home and at school				helping and supporting others
Learning skills	increasingly able to learn as part of a group becoming an independent learner accessing information from books and the computer						

Figure 2. An overview of developmental progress from eleven to sixteen years in children with Down syndrome

the next section general trends and some important influences on teenagers' development are considered, based on the authors' research studies.

Major trends in development

There is a very wide range of variation in the rates of progress of teenagers with Down syndrome. The authors have conducted two in-depth studies of the development of teenagers with Down syndrome, aged from 11-20 years, and the detailed information on the range of skills achieved is included in the practical modules in this series for the guidance of parents and teachers. For example, the specific information on the range of achievements in reading and writing is included in the reading module, on number, time and money in the number modules and on speech and language skills in the speech and language module. The detailed information on practical self-help skills and social behaviour is in the social module. The information on health, puberty and sexuality is discussed in the health section of this module on page 35.

In this section, an overview of the findings is presented as they illustrate important progression with age for almost every skill measured and also some strengths and weaknesses in specific areas of development. The data also allows the progress of teenagers who have been included in mainstream schooling for the whole of their education to be compared with the progress of teenagers who have been in special education settings. The authors conducted surveys of teenagers with Down syndrome in the same county in the UK in 1987 and in 1999. This has enabled them to compare the progress of two different cohorts of teenagers to see if there has been any improvement in educational or social outcomes as a result of changes in social attitudes and expectation and improvements in educational opportunities over the 12 year period. In 1987, the authors collected information on 90 teenagers in the county of Hampshire, UK.[3] At this time they were all being educated in special schools for children with severe learning difficulties.

In 1999, the authors and colleagues collected information on the progress of 46 teenagers in the same county, where the full inclusion of children with Down syndrome into local mainstream schools from 5 years of age began in one part of the county in 1988. This inclusion project was supported by charitable funding and inclusion did not begin at the same time in the rest of the county. This has enabled a comparative study of the progress of teenagers with Down syndrome, of similar abilities and family backgrounds, placed in full inclusion or in special schools, purely on the basis of where they lived. This study is reported in full elsewhere,[1,2] but it is important to note that the teenagers in the two groups do not vary on any significant family or social variables which might affect their progress.

In 1999, data was originally collected from 28 teenagers in special schools but to try to ensure that we were comparing young people of potentially similar abilities, the 5 'least able' teenagers from the special schools were taken out of the comparison group, before these figures were calculated and compared. These 5 'least able' teenagers are those with significantly more developmental delay and health problems than the rest of the group. Two of them have autism in addition to Down syndrome and three of the five have significantly high rates of difficult behaviours. These young people have had multiple difficulties since childhood, and children with this level of difficulty would not have been placed in mainstream classes in any part of the county at the time of the study. In the view of the authors, the needs of this group and their families are significantly different from those of the majority of teenagers with Down syndrome, and this issue is addressed in more detail on page 24. The average age of the mainstream group is also two years younger than the average age of the special school group, which would reduce the likelihood of finding higher scores on any measures for the total mainstream group.

See also:
- An overview of less typical developmental issues in Down syndrome [DSii-01-09]

It is also important to note that the teenagers in the mainstream schools have been fully included in age-appropriate classes in their local schools, supported by a Learning Support Assistant for the majority of the day. They have not been in special classes or resource rooms in mainstream schools and, usually, they have been the only child with Down syndrome or a similar level of learning difficulty in school until they reached secondary schools. In secondary school some have continued to be the only teenager with Down syndrome, but some have been with one or two others with Down syndrome in school.

Many of the results of the study were not as the researchers might have predicted and the findings raise some important issues for parents and edu-

An overview of the development of teenagers with Down syndrome

cators of teenagers with Down syndrome to consider and to address.

In both 1987 and 1999, the information was collected by surveys. In both studies, parents completed a questionnaire designed by the authors, the Sacks & Buckley Questionnaire (SBQ). In the second study, additional standardised questionnaires were also used, the Vineland Adaptive Behaviour Scale (VABS)[9] and the Conners Rating Scales (CRS).[10] The two main questionnaires (the SBQ and VABS) both contain measures of personal independence skills - Daily Living Skills - which include measures of skills in dressing, toileting, bathing, cleaning, laundry and meal preparation, also time, money, telephone use and road safety. They also both contain measures of speech, language and literacy skills - Communication Skills, and measures of friendship, leisure and social skills - Socialisation Skills. The Vineland Adaptive Behaviour Scale provides normative data which allows scores achieved on the scales to be translated into age equivalent scores. This is useful because it allows us to compare the progress of the teenagers in different aspects of their development. We would expect progress to be even for most individuals, that is, that all skills will be at approximately the same age-level. The age equivalent score also allow us to identify the extent of progress with age and this is illustrated in the first set of histograms in Figure 3.

Progress with age

These findings are presented separately for the teenagers in mainstream and special schools, as some interesting and important similarities and differences which are of practical significance emerge as we consider the findings.

The first two histograms in Figure 3 indicate that Daily Living Skills and Socialisation Skills can be expected to improve significantly as young people with Down syndrome progress through their teens (though with the caution that these figures are for different teenagers in each age group not the same teenagers as they get older). However, as we also demonstrated progression with age on all measures in the 1987 study, we are confident that the majority of young people with Down syndrome will progress their skills during their teenage years. When we look at the third histogram in Figure 3, for Communication Skills, we see significant progress for the oldest group of mainstreamed teenagers but no significant progress with age for the teenagers in special education. These differences in progress in speech, language and literacy will explored in more detail in the next section.

The first important conclusion we can draw from this piece of research is that we can expect significant progress in all areas of development during teenage years. There is no evidence for a 'plateau' being reached, or even a slowing of progress.

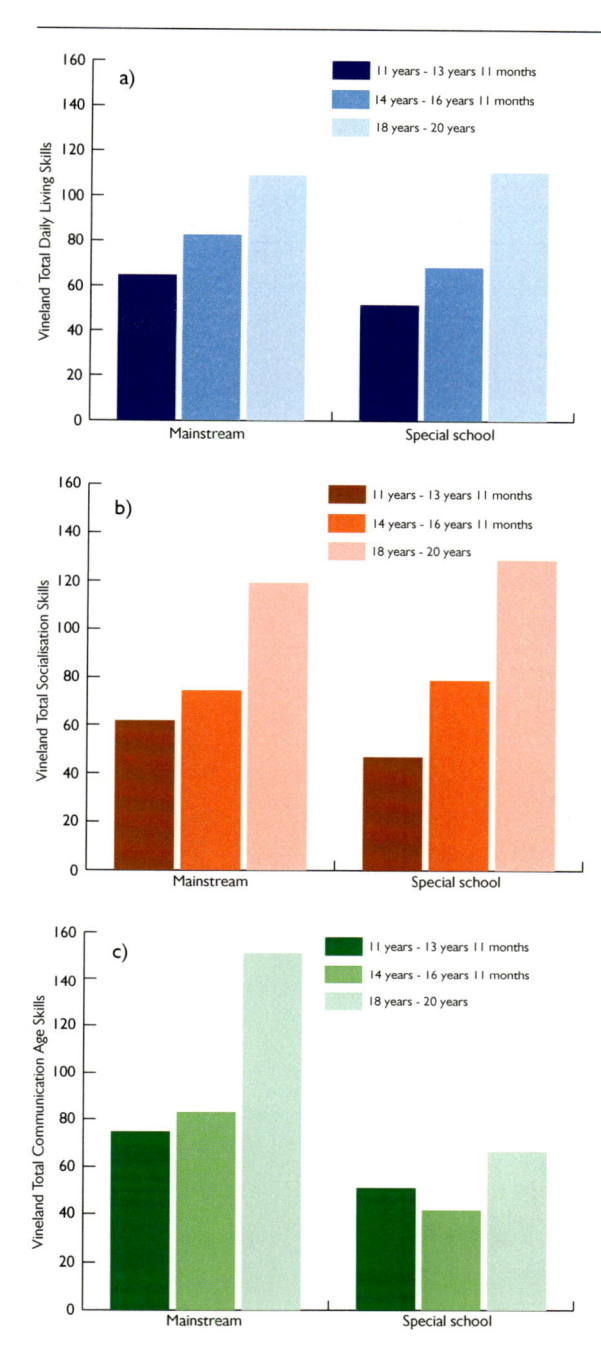

Figure 3. Progress with age for Daily Living Skills, Socialisation and Communication Skills (group means for Vineland Age Equivalent Scores)

An overview of the development of teenagers with Down syndrome

The reader will also have observed that there are no significant overall differences in the Daily Living Skills or Socialisation Skills of the teenagers educated in special or mainstream schools, though there is a difference on one measure which contributes to the Socialisation Skills score - the Interpersonal Relationships Scale. This difference may be important and is discussed in more detail in the next section and on page 21.

A more detailed look

For each main scale on the VABS there are 3 subscales which contribute to that score and the information for these subscales is illustrated in Figure 4. The first histogram illustrates that for Daily Living Skills the teenagers were performing at a similar level in personal and practical skills in the domestic (e.g. preparing meals, cleaning, taking care of laundry), personal (e.g. independence in toileting, bathing, dressing) and community (e.g. staying at home alone, time, money, telephone and road skills) areas. It also illustrates that there were no significant differences in outcomes for the teenagers from the mainstream or the special schools.

The second histogram, however, illustrates that for the Socialisation Skills measure there is a difference on the subscales for the interpersonal relationships subscale, which covers social interaction, dating and friendship skills. There were no differences on the play and leisure (going to clubs, games, hobbies, leisure activities) or on the coping skills (awareness of manners, social sensitivity and social rules) subscales.

On the interpersonal relationships subscale, the teenagers educated in the special schools scored significantly higher, largely due to differences in scores for the oldest of the age groups. This was the only measure of the many measure used in this research which showed a significantly better outcome for teenagers in special education. The numbers of teenagers in the study are quite small - 18 in mainstream education and 23 in special education - so that further research is needed to explore any significance of this finding further. However, one possibility is that the teenagers in special education have had more opportunity to develop mutually supportive, reciprocal friendships with peers of similar abilities and interests than those included in mainstream schools.

The third histogram in Figure 4 illustrates the results for the three subscales in the Communication Skills score. For the teenagers in mainstream schools, the results indicate that their receptive and expressive language is progressing at the same rate and that reading and writing is a specific strength and better than might be predicted from their other language abilities. For the teenagers in special education, their receptive language is at a similar level to those in mainstream school but their expressive language is, in fact, developmentally 3 years behind their receptive language. Their reading and writing abilities are at the same level as their receptive language

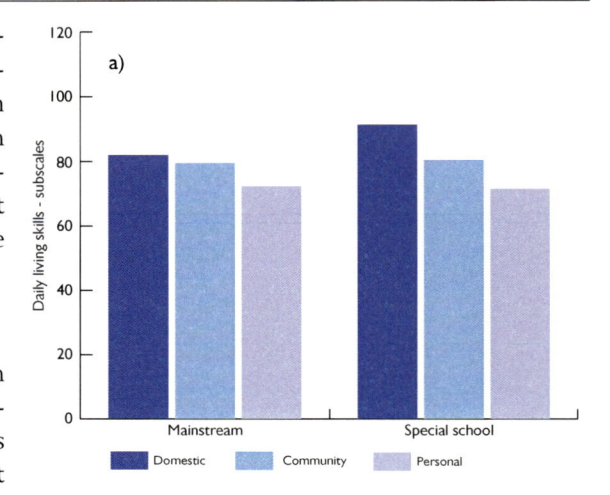

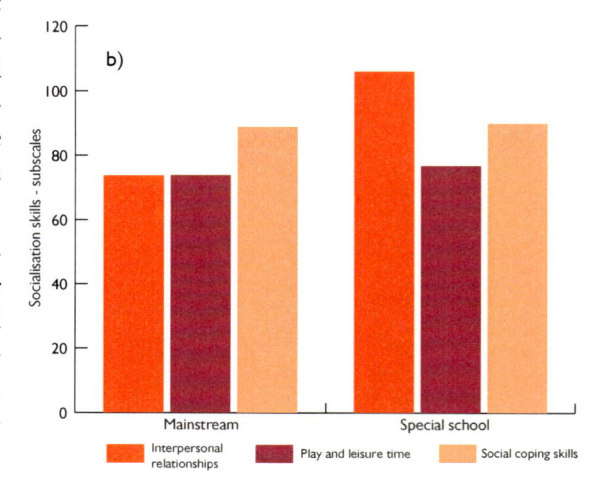

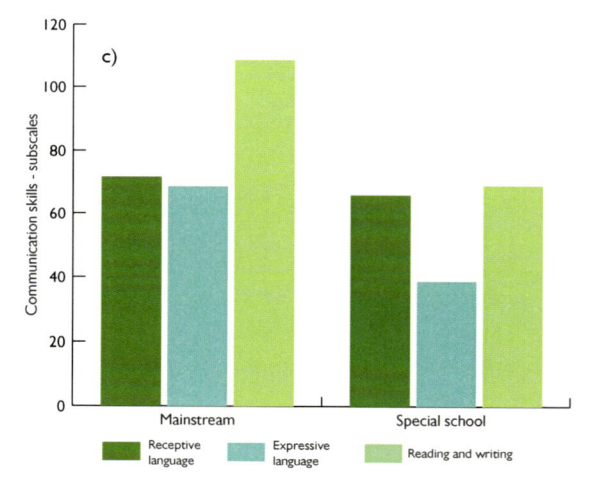

Figure 4. The relationships between the subscales for Daily Living, Socialisation and Communication skills (group means for Vineland Age Equivalent Scores)

but significantly behind the reading and writing skills of the mainstreamed teenagers (by approximately 3 years).

It is possible that the improved expressive language of the teenagers in mainstream schools is linked to their reading and writing progress. Researchers suggest that expressive skills are delayed by hearing, speech motor difficulties, auditory memory and auditory processing difficulties.[11-13] Therefore, written language may well be easier for young people with Down syndrome to access and to learn vocabulary and grammar from than spoken language. In addition, phonics work plus reading practice may improve speech-motor production skills and speech intelligibility.

The teenagers being educated in mainstream classrooms, with the individual help of a Learning Support Assistant, will have received daily literacy teaching with their typically developing peers. They will also have recorded their learning in all lessons by writing it down and reading it - with whatever level of support was needed. The level of engagement in literacy activities will have been much greater than that experienced in the special school classrooms.

Overall profiles

In Figure 5 the histograms show the overall results for the main developmental areas - Daily Living, Socialisation and Communication Skills. For the teenagers in the mainstream schools there are no significant differences in the progress being made in each of these areas of development. Communication Skills are good, largely due to their progress with expressive language and literacy. For the teenagers in the special schools, their Communication Skills are significantly delayed relative to their Daily Living and Socialisation skills.

This special school profile is, in fact, the one that researchers would expect to see for teenagers with Down syndrome. A number of studies have found that speech and language skills, particularly expressive skills are specifically delayed relative to both non-verbal cognitive abilities and to social and independence skills.[13,14]

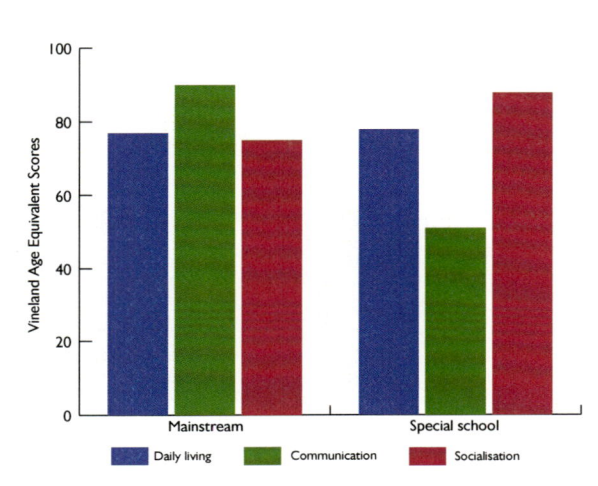

Figure 5. The relationship between the three aspects of development, Daily Living, Communication and Socialisation (group means for Vineland Age Equivalent Scores)

The results of the current research with the Hampshire teenagers suggests that it is possible to remediate the speech and language difficulties and to bring expressive language abilities in line with receptive language for teenagers with Down syndrome. The results indicate that a major factor may be the development of reading and writing and the use of literacy activities to teach and to support spoken language development.

Another major factor may be that the mainstreamed teenagers have been surrounded by typically developing competent spoken language users since they entered preschools at 3 years of age and this spoken language and communication environment will have been very different to that experienced by the teenagers in the special schools. Almost all of the special school group have been in special schools for children with severe learning difficulties for their entire school career and this means that they have been with children the majority of whom have very significantly impaired language.

Personality and behaviour

Another major area of developmental importance that was looked at in these Hampshire teenage studies was the extent of behaviour difficulties, whether any behaviour difficulties change with age and if school placement has any influence on behaviour. In the authors' experience, behaviour can be an important issue in teenage and adult years for some individuals.

Significantly difficult behaviour affects the learning and social opportunities of a teenager with Down syndrome and can create considerable stress for teachers and for families. Conversely, teenagers who can behave in a socially acceptable and competent manner will be more likely to have friends, to have active social lives and to be successful in work as adults, than those who do not.

In the authors' experience, socially confident and acceptable behaviour can be more important in determining quality of life for adults than academic achievements. Of course, both contribute to increasing the range of opportunities and independence open to adults, but skills and abilities without behaviour control will not lead to a happy life. This is equally true, of course, for non-disabled teenagers and adults.

Difficult behaviours need to be considered in relation to the helpful and socially sensitive behaviour and the positive personalities that are characteristic of most teenagers with Down syndrome. Many references to the positive aspects of teenagers personalities were made by parents during the recent Hampshire survey, for example:-

"J is a happy and content girl, very understanding, helpful and has a great personality - she brings out the best in everyone."

"He is happy and outgoing and lots of people know him so we talk to more people because of him."

"She is a wonderful, happy and most loved member of our family. She is kind, caring, happy and thoughtful."

"A has a positive approach to life and brings that to the family. His caring nature and enthusiasm are infectious. I think he has made the family dynamics easier than they would have been, especially teenage years."

"She is good company, always happy, funny and content"

"Good point is he is a happy lad who is good fun and has taught us a lot".

"Very loving, trusting and happy boy - enjoys life and is very sociable."

"Our daughter brings more love, fun and laughter to family life and though she will never be 'academic' there are other qualities she has which cannot be measured."

"He is popular, friendly and non-judgemental…he has added another dimension to our lives".

"Brings a lot of happiness to our lives. Her disruptiveness - being rude or awkward- can cause parents and sister to get cross and upset"

The last quote highlights the fact that difficult behaviours occur only sometimes and do not define the person's character. Someone with a positive personality can be difficult at times and this would characterise most of the teenagers in the survey. However, this does not mean the difficult behav-

An overview of the development of teenagers with Down syndrome

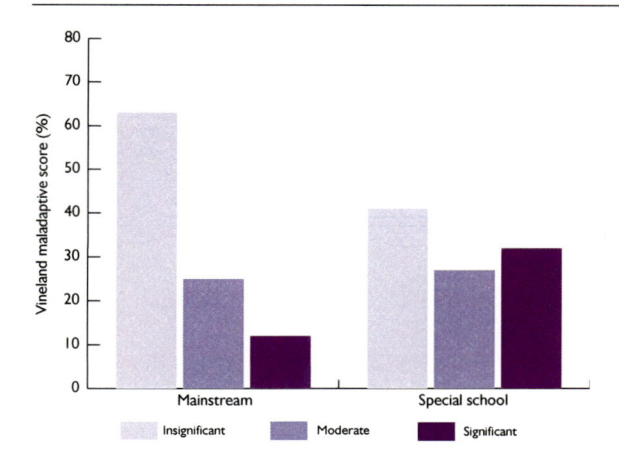

Figure 6. The significance of reported behaviour difficulties (percentage of teenagers in each category)

iours are not distressing when they do occur and most parents are pleased to obtain advice on how to handle them.

Several measures were used to collect information about any behaviour difficulties that the teenagers had. There were behaviour questions on the original Sacks and Buckley Questionnaire[3] and a Maladaptive Behaviour Scale on the Vineland Adaptive Behaviour Scales.[9] In addition, the Conners Behaviour Rating Scale[10] provides measures of several different aspects of behavioural difficulties, hyperactivity, cognitive problems or inattention, oppositional behaviour and Attention Deficit/Hyperactivity Disorder-ADHD.

All the measures illustrated that difficult behaviours tend to improve with age for most individuals, with only one teenager over 18 years in the main schools comparison group having even a moderate level of difficulties. This strongly suggests that many of the behaviours reported for the younger teenagers may be linked to general cognitive delays and immaturity.

There was only one measure on which the teenagers from the different school systems scored significantly differently - The VABS Maladaptive Behaviour Scale - and these results are illustrated in Figure 6. The scores can be classified in terms of the severity of the behaviour difficulties. As the data below shows, significant behaviour difficulties only affect a minority. The teenagers in the mainstream schools were less likely to have difficulties, with 63% having no significant difficulties compared with 41% in the special schools, 25% having a moderate level of difficulties compared with 27% in the special schools and 12% (one in eight) having significant behaviour difficulties compared with 32% (one in three) in special schools.

The reader is reminded that the 5 'least able' teenagers in the special schools are not included in this comparison. Three of these 5 had very high scores for difficult behaviours and the remaining 2 had low scores.

This means that in the whole sample of teenagers, and the whole sample is representative of all teenagers with Down syndrome, 26% (one in four) have some significant behaviour difficulties which will be probably causing problems at home and at school on a daily basis.

The Vineland Maladaptive Behaviour Scale predominantly includes questions about two main types of behaviour, those that may reflect anxiety and nervousness and those that reflect conduct disorder and poor attention.

On the specific Conners Behaviour measures which focus on conduct disorders and attention difficulties, there were no significant differences between the levels of difficulties for the teenagers in mainstream or special schools. When the scores of the teenagers with Down syndrome are compared with norms for typically developing teenagers, the proportion of the total group who had serious difficulties was 16% on each of the Oppositional Behaviour, the Cognitive problems/inattention and the ADHD measure and 37% on the Hyperactivity measure. (The reader should note that some 5% of the regular population of teenagers of the same age will score in the serious difficulties range as defined by the Conners Scales). Some behaviours may reflect immaturity and improve with age.

An overview of the development of teenagers with Down syndrome

The hyperactivity measures include, being always 'on the go', hard to control while shopping, runs about or climbs excessively in situations where it is inappropriate, restless in the squirmy sense, has difficulty waiting in line or taking turns, has difficulty playing or engaging in leisure activities quietly. The high score here may reflect immaturity for age. Similar findings have been reported by other researchers and interpreted in this way.[15,16]

For example, in another UK research study which included four groups, children and teenagers with Down syndrome, their brothers and sisters, other children with learning disabilities and typically developing children, the hyperactivity score of the 16-19 year olds with Down syndrome was the same as that of the typically developing group whose mean age was 9 years 4 months and included 4 to 15 year olds. In this study the behaviour rating scores all significantly and steadily declined with age from 4 to 19 years for the children and teenagers with Down syndrome.[16]

Behaviour is good relative to cognitive abilities

As reported in other studies, all the behaviour scores for the group with Down syndrome were significantly lower than those for the children with a similar level of learning difficulties but not Down syndrome, but tended to be higher than the scores of the two non-disabled groups, brothers and sisters of those with Down syndrome and a typically developing group from the general population.[16] Readers may be interested to know that the behaviour scores of the brothers and sisters of children and teenagers with Down syndrome were no different from those of children from the general population who did not have a disabled brother or sister. Therefore, there was no evidence of adverse effects of growing up with a sibling with Down syndrome.

Some researchers report that more boys than girls have difficult behaviour but in the authors' study there were no differences between boys and girls, in either the mainstream or special school groups, on any of the measures and an Australian study also found no general differences.[17]

The link between behaviour and poor communication skills

Similar to other studies, and the authors' 1986 study, there was a significant relationship between expressive communication skills and behaviour difficulties - the more limited a teenager's expressive language ability, the more likely he or she is to have behaviour difficulties. The implication here is that at least some difficult behaviours are the teenager's way of communicating when he/she does not have the language to do so. In addition, some behaviours may be the result of the frustration that arises when an individual is not understood.

Difficult behaviour is stressful for families

Many studies report a link between family stress and the level of difficult behaviours, with mothers often particularly affected.[18-20] Therefore, while only a minority of teenagers with Down syndrome can be described as difficult, it is important that the needs of these young people and their families are recognised. Many, if not most, difficult behaviours can be changed but not always easily or quickly. More persistent difficult behaviours will be more difficult to change and families and teachers will benefit from the support of professionals skilled in behaviour management.

Behaviour difficulties can arise for a variety of reasons and, because of the effects that they have on the life of affected teenagers, there is a prac-

> **See also:**
> - Strategies for changing behaviour and developing social skills for individuals with Down syndrome [DSii-14-09]

> **See also:**
> - Social development for individuals with Down syndrome - An overview [DSii-14-01]
> - Social development for teenagers with Down syndrome (11-16 years) [DSii-14-04]

tical module for this age group which discusses causes and management approaches for difficult behaviours in depth.

In summary

In summary, when we look at the main trends in the data we see:

- steady progress with age, and no evidence of a plateau in any area of development.

- progress in independence in daily living skills and in social skills - and no significant difference in progress for these in mainstream or special education settings, perhaps because a major influence on progress in these areas of development is the learning opportunities and expectations of the family.

- significantly greater delay in expressive communication skills when compared with progress in daily living and social skills for the teenagers educated in special schools.

- no significant delay in expressive communication skills for the teenagers educated in mainstream schools. This means that the teenagers in mainstream schools have significantly better spoken language and literacy skills than their similar ability peers in special education. They also have significantly better numeracy skills. The main benefit of inclusive education of the type experienced by these teenagers has been in spoken language and academic progress.

- while general social and social independence skills did not vary between the two groups, the teenagers in special schools had significantly better interpersonal friendship skills, and the importance of this finding and some of the reasons for it are discussed more fully in the next section.

- the majority of parents described the positive personalities of their teenagers, their social sensitivity, and how much they contributed to family life. However, about 16% of teenagers do exhibit difficult behaviours at times, and about one third show some immature behaviour for their age (but probably not immature for their cognitive and communication abilities at this time). Most teenagers will grow out of these behaviours by their late teens.

- a small number of teenagers do show persistent difficult behaviours, and this reduces their social and learning opportunities as well as increasing the stress experienced by their families.

- about 10% of any population of individuals with Down syndrome can be expected to have profound and multiple disabilities. Life for these teenagers and their families is rather different than for the rest of the population. They are still highly dependent and their educational and support needs are different. Parents of these teenagers frequently express the view that their needs are not understood, especially by those representing the majority of individuals with Down syndrome, such as Down syndrome associations, and by those campaigning for inclusive education. The needs of these individuals is explored in more detail on page 25 and in a separate module *An overview of less typical developmental issues in Down syndrome*.[DSii-10-09]

An overview of the development of teenagers with Down syndrome

What levels of achievement can we expect?

The previous section has identified some of the main trends in achievements and factors which may influence them, but does not give the reader an idea of the actual skills that teenagers with Down syndrome may have in each area of development or the range of individual differences. Taking each of the headings in Figure 2 (page 7) the range of expected achievements are summarised in this section, based on the Hampshire surveys of representative groups of teenagers.

Personal care and daily living skills

Personal care and hygiene

Most teenagers with Down syndrome are well on the way to personal independence and privacy in the area of self care. Almost all teenagers (some 85%) can dress and undress without assistance and manage most fastenings. A similar number can choose and find their own clothes each day and some 70% can choose appropriate clothes for the weather. Most teenagers (some 85%) choose their own new clothes and show a preference for fashion styles.

However, only about half the group are completely independent when we consider personal hygiene as, while 92% can wash in the bath unaided and some 80% dry themselves unaided, only half of the teenagers can run a bath without help, only a third could wash their hair without help and only 10% could cut their own nails. Almost everyone was fully continent day and night (95%) and could go to the toilet without a prompt. However while some 90% could manage their clothing unaided in the toilet, 25% were still receiving assistance to wipe themselves, and 20% did not flush the toilet. While 65% washed their own hands without help, 20% did not - this means that some 25% of the teenagers still needed assistance in the toilet.

Almost everyone could clean their teeth and brush their hair unaided, but less than half actually did brush their hair daily without help, presumably because parents felt that they could improve their teenager's appearance if they still helped. This raises the issue of encouraging independence. Parents need to be very aware of the importance of being independent for self-esteem and personal growth. It is not easy to let go and to accept that, while teenagers are learning to be competent they will not make as good a job of the tasks as when parents do them, but they will only reach a good level of competence if allowed to try for themselves.

It is easy to continue to provide help for 11 and 12 year olds without considering what is age-appropriate and the need to begin to encourage independence and privacy. Most teenagers with Down syndrome will need more practice to become competent and therefore this should start early. The shower is often easier to manage than the bath, especially for washing hair and rinsing it adequately. Nail clippers are easier to learn to use than scissors, and learning to be fully independent in the toilet takes time and practice.

In each area, teenagers need to begin to take over the tasks over a period of time, with parents teaching them how to do the tasks rather than doing them for them.

Mealtimes and cooking

Almost all teenagers (95%) could eat and drink completely independently though some 30% still needed assistance with cutting up food. Almost everyone (95%) could serve themselves from serving dishes on the table and 90% could help themselves to salt, pepper and sauces. Everyone could be taken out to eat in a restaurant. When it comes to making meals and snacks, everyone could help themselves to a biscuit, 95% could get a glass of water, some 64% could make squash and 82% could get a glass of milk without assistance. Half of the teenagers could make a sandwich, a piece of toast and a cup of tea or coffee. About a third of the teenagers could use a can opener, about 25% could use the microwave oven and only 10% could use the grill or the oven. In other words, beyond simple snacks, most teenagers could not prepare or cook a meal. However, most of them (80%) could lay and clear the table and about half could wash and dry the crockery.

Learning to prepare and cook meals involves taking risks, using knives, hot pans, boiling water, grills, open gas or electric rings and hot ovens. However, in later teens, some young people become very skilled in cooking and many take catering courses. Like learning to carry out all personal hygiene tasks, teenagers will only learn to cook safely if they are able to learn the necessary skills, in small steps and with supervision.

Independence and responsibility in the home

Most teenagers (86%) had their own bedroom and 65% - 70% took a pride in their room and kept it tidy. Almost all (90%) put up their own pictures and posters. Some 14% of teenagers helped with household chores. However, in terms of being able to be left alone at home, about a third of teenagers could be safely left for short periods of time but only 7% for longer periods.

Most teenagers had the privacy of a room of their own, and were beginning to take some responsibility for tidying. We did not ask about doing the laundry or ironing, but most teenagers should be encouraged to learn all the domestic tasks which will enable them to care for their own rooms, laundry and shared areas in the house as they approach adulthood.

The main reasons that parents give for not leaving teenagers alone for long is their limited ability to deal with the unexpected. Most teenagers could be trusted not to do anything inappropriate or dangerous if left alone, but most teenagers could not yet use the telephone independently to call for help in an emergency. Some families were extending the time the teenager could be left alone in the house by enlisting the help of neighbours. If a neighbour is at home, the teenager can go to them for help if it is needed.

Social independence outside the home

Of the mainstream teenagers, 22% could go to a local shop alone, 83% had pocket money, 44% could cross roads alone and only one teenager walked to the school bus alone. Of the special school teenagers, 30% could go to a local shop alone, 65% had pocket money, 35% could cross roads alone and 13% walked to the school or work bus alone. It was only the oldest teenagers (over 17) that were travelling about independently in the community.

This means that most teenagers could not travel about the local neighbourhood without supervision. Learning to be independent in the community is another area that involves risk taking. However, the necessary skills will only be learned if a teaching programme is planned and the young person able to

> **See also:**
> - Social development for teenagers with Down syndrome (11-16 years) [DSii-14-04]

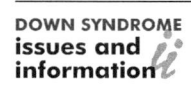

learn over a period of time, in small steps. For example, when crossing the road, a teenager can be encouraged to identify the right place to cross - usually a proper pedestrian crossing with lights to stop the traffic - can press the light and be in control of deciding when to cross, while still being accompanied by an adult or another teenager. Similarly, bus skills can be learned by allowing the teenager to take the lead in asking for the fare and handing over the money, with an adult in the background to help if necessary. Slowly, the support can be faded in small steps.

For some teenagers, the use of a mobile 'phone will aid their safety and independence - and reassure parents that they are safe. Important numbers can be stored so that they can be dialled with one key press if the teenager needs assistance.

The level of independence attained during the teenage years will vary considerably between individuals, and most young people with Down syndrome will continue to develop their independence significantly during their young adult life.

The reader may be interested to note that there was no significant difference in the personal or social independence skills of teenagers in mainstream or special schools and there was no significant improvement for teenagers in 1999 compared to teenagers in 1987. When we wrote about the findings of the 1987 survey, we encouraged parents to raise their expectations but we have little evidence that this has happened.

Motor skills

In the 1999 survey, everyone is able to walk, to climb stairs with one foot on each step and some 90% of teenagers can jump with both feet together and hop on one foot. Everyone can throw and kick a ball and almost everyone (96%) can catch a ball. Almost all teenagers (93%) can swim without aids and ride a tricycle, with 36% able to ride a bicycle. We did not ask about the range of other sporting activities that teenagers may be skilled in but we know that some teenagers are skilled at gymnastics, horse riding, diving, skiing, baseball and football and that these activities are an important part of their lives.

> **See also:**
> - Motor skills development for individuals with Down syndrome - an overview [DSii-12-01] and
> - Motor skills development for teenagers with Down syndrome (11-16 years) [DSii-12-04]

We would encourage all parents and teachers to support teenagers in a wide range of physical activities for two reasons, health and opportunities for social contacts and friendships.

About half of all teenagers are considered overweight by their parents, and this tendency to weight gain, which is more significant after puberty, can be reduced by taking sufficient exercise as well as by healthy eating. Exercise will also improve gait and posture, breathing and general fitness.

In addition, taking part in sporting activities can bring teenagers into contact with peers - both other peers with disabilities and typically developing peers. We have already suggested that this is important for social and emotional development.

Speech and Language

The communication skills of most teenagers, that is their ability to get their message across, is very good. Almost all teenagers (96%) could start conversations, participate in conversations, talk about past and future events, ask questions and use the telephone. However, getting the message across can be supported by actions and gestures, facial expressions and tones of voice and the listener's knowledge of the context and topic of the message. Almost all teenagers with Down syndrome have some speech delays and difficulties, that is, their speech is not as clear, fluent and easy to understand as that of their non-disabled peers. Some 33% were reported to have difficulty being understood by those unfamiliar with them such as assistants in shops or restaurants.

In addition to the effect of speech phonology and articulation difficulties, the intelligibility of their messages will also be reduced because they are often not able to produce fully grammatically complete sentences. All the teenagers in the 1999 study were talking whereas in 1986 there were 3 teenagers in a sample of 90 with no speech at all . There were significant differences between the spoken language skills of the teenagers in mainstream education and those in special education settings. All the teenagers in the mainstream schools usually used sentences of 5 or more words but only 61% of those in the special schools. Some 40% of the teenagers in special education settings mainly used shorter 3 or 4 word utterances to communicate, some 13% mainly only one or two words and half used 'key-word' or 'telegraphic' utterances - leaving out the grammatical words and word endings and using mainly verbs, nouns and adjectives.

Most teenagers understand more spoken language than they can use in their own expressive language. This is a very frustrating situation for them and it also often leads to the understanding of teenagers being underestimated. Importantly, the receptive language of the teenagers in the special education classrooms was not more delayed - only their expressive skills were significantly behind those of the mainstreamed teenagers. This suggests that some aspects of the inclusive education situation was enabling teenagers with Down syndrome to overcome some of the typical expressive language difficulties. One factor that the authors believe to be important is the extent of inclusion in literacy activities, where the outcomes for the two school systems are also different as described in the next section.

See also:
- Memory development for individuals with Down syndrome [DSii-05-01]

See also:
- Speech and language development for individuals with Down syndrome - an overview [DSii-03-01] and
- Speech and language development for teenagers with Down syndrome (11-16 years) [DSii-03-06]

Only 40% of all teenagers were reported to be using more than 10 signs to communicate, though 60% were reported to understand more than 10 signs. Some 77% of the parents of the teenagers who used signs found them helpful. It is likely that most teenagers can improve their speech and language skills, and practical advice on how to assess their individual needs and improve speech intelligibility, vocabulary, sentences and communication skills is covered in the *Speech and language development for teenagers with Down syndrome* module.[DSii-03-06]

Reading and writing

All the teenagers in mainstream education were able to read and could read short sentences and simple books - simple in the sense of containing simple sentence structures - but with age-appropriate content and interest. Almost all (94%) of the teenagers in mainstream schools could read more than 50 words and simple instructions, 83% could read items in the newspaper and 78% read for pleasure. All the teenagers in this group knew the names of the letters of the alphabet, 89% knew all the letter sounds, 78% could sound out words when reading and 72% could sound out words for spelling.

The reading achievements of the teenagers in special education were significantly behind those of their mainstream peers. Some 78% could read something and of this group, 83% could read their own name and some 'social sight' words (usually words with environmental and practical values such as 'ladies', 'gents', 'bus-stop', 'exit', 'police'). Some 39% of the readers could read more than 50 words and read simple books, 22% could read items in the newspaper, 48% could read simple instructions and 35% read for pleasure. Some 50% of the special education teenagers know the names of all the letters of the alphabet, 41% know the letter sounds, 32% can 'sound out' words when reading and 23% can 'sound out' words when spelling.

When writing skills are considered, 90% of all the teenagers could trace over and copy letters and words and almost everyone (93%) could write their name. Of the teenagers in the mainstream schools, 94% could write their family names, 83% could write simple sentences and 61% could write their own address, simple messages, simple stories and a short letter. Of the teenagers in the special schools, 48% could write their family names, 30% could write simple sentences and their own address, 17% could write simple messages, 4% could write simple stories and 22% a short letter.

The reading skills of most teenagers can be developed further during their teenage years and some may begin to read at this time. The 11-16 Reading and writing module contains detailed information on how to extend the reading and writing skills of teenagers, and how to make even limited reading abilities relevant and useful.

> **See also:**
> - *Reading and writing for individuals with Down syndrome - an overview* [DSii-07-01] and
> - *Reading and writing for teenagers with Down syndrome (11-16 years)* [DSii-07-05]

Number, money and time

Overall, the arithmetic skills of the teenagers educated in mainstream schools tend to be significantly ahead of the teenagers in the special schools but not their money skills. All the teenagers in the mainstream schools could recite the numbers to 20 accurately and 94% could count objects to 20 and do simple addition with numbers within this range. Half of this group could recite the numbers to 50 and a third could count more than 20 objects accurately and recite numbers accurately to 100. While all the teenagers could add simple numbers, 78% could complete simple subtraction, 28% could complete simple multiplication and 17% could complete simple division.

For the teenagers in the special schools the figures indicate that 69% could recite the numbers to 20 accurately and 52% could count objects to 20 and 61% could do simple addition. Some 26% of this group could recite the numbers to 50, 17% could count more than 20 objects accurately and 13% could recite numbers accurately to 100. While more than half of the teenagers could add simple numbers, 43% could complete simple subtraction, 4% could complete simple multiplication and 4% could complete simple division.

When we consider money skills, all but one of the teenagers relied on shop assistants to take correct sums of money. The special school teenagers tend to be doing better with 48% able to count simple amounts of money and 26% able to give an approximately appropriate amount in a shop, compared with 33% and 11% of teenagers in mainstream schools who could do these tasks.

When we consider general knowledge of time, only 20% of the teenagers could tell the time completely, all the teenagers in the mainstream schools could name the days of the week, and give their own name and age, 94% could say their own address, 89% their birthday, and 61% could name the months of the year. For the teenagers in the special schools 70% could name

An overview of the development of teenagers with Down syndrome

> **See also:**
> - Number skills for individuals with Down syndrome - an overview [DSii-09-01] and
> - Number skills for teenagers with Down syndrome (11-16 years) [DSii-09-04]

the days of the week, all could give their own name and 87% their age, 65% could say their own address and 43% their birthday and 35% could name the months of the year.

The 11-16 Number module contains a wide range of activities to develop number, money and time skills for teenagers. It encourages parents and teachers to continue to develop a basic understanding of the number system and simple calculations, as well as providing tips for supporting functional use of time and money.

Social and interpersonal development

Leisure interests

If we consider leisure interest and activities, watching TV was the favourite and some 80% of teenagers watched TV often, 55% were interested in pop-stars, 74% were interested in pop music. Some 40% of mainstreamed teenagers and 70% of those from special schools listened to pop music often. Some 44% of mainstreamed teenagers were interested in sports, 33% interested in the cinema and 22% in fashion, with 70% of those from special schools interested in sport, 65% interested in the cinema and 43% interested in fashion. If we consider more passive activities, some 35% read often, 38% played games often, and 27% of mainstreamed teenagers and 48% of those from special schools often enjoyed drawing. Some of the group differences may be due to the fact that there are more older teenagers (over 18 years) in the special school group. This list of interests and activities includes many that are age-appropriate but the teenagers tended to be engaged in these at home on their own, especially as many had TVs and computers in their own rooms. All but one teenager could operate the TV independently and 80% could operate computer games.

Friends

Some 58% of all the teenagers spend time with friends at least once a week. When we asked about these friends, 18% of the teenagers from the mainstream schools and 64% of the teenagers from the special schools had *only* disabled friends. Some 47% of the teenagers from mainstream schools and 9% of those from special schools had only non-disabled friends. About a third of all the teenagers had both disabled and non-disabled friends

This figures indicate that about 50% of the teenagers educated in mainstream schools had no disabled friends and that 64% of the teenagers educated in special schools had no non-disabled friends.

The information provided on the sort of clubs attended partly explains these friendship patterns, as 55% of the mainstream teenagers and 43% of teenagers from specials schools belong to 'mainstream' clubs, and 65% of the mainstream teenagers and 56 % of teenagers from special schools belong to 'special clubs'. There was apparently the opportunity for more teenagers to have both disabled and non-disabled friends, as for example 65% of mainstream teenagers attended 'special' clubs but 18% did not make 'special' friends there.

However, the information suggests that 35% of the mainstream teenagers *never* had the opportunity to make friends with disabled peers in or out of school and that some 57% of the teenagers attending special schools had little opportunity to make friends with non-disabled peers in or out of school.

Information provided on going to parties and discos supports the above picture. While 69% of teenagers from mainstream education are invited to discos and parties organised for typical peers, only 16% of the teenagers from special schools receive such invitations. Some 80% of all teenagers go to discos and parties and some 40% go as often as every month, indicating that the groups of teenagers have equally active social lives but that those in mainstream education are more likely to go to inclusive or 'ordinary' social events and those teenagers from special schools are more likely to be going to 'special' events. The teenagers' social world and friendships are being strongly affected by school placements.

In the authors' view these findings have negative implications for both groups of teenagers. The teenagers being educated with their disabled peers seem to have little opportunity to socialise in inclusive or non-disabled settings and are less likely to have non-disabled friends. This is likely to put them at a disadvantage in feeling at ease with and being able to communicate with non-disabled peers when they attend inclusive further education colleges, when they are in the workplace and when they are out and about in the community.

In contrast, the teenagers educated in mainstream schools seem to be at risk of not having the opportunity to have friends with a similar level of disability for the close, special friendships and to find boy friends and girlfriend. Some 38% of the teenagers from the special schools had boyfriends or girlfriends yet no one from the mainstream schools had a boyfriend or girlfriend at the time of the survey.

The effects of these social experiences during the early teenage years from 11 to 16 seems to have a possibly serious consequence for some of them once they leave school. We only have a small number of older teenagers (over 17 years) who have left a mainstream school, but they seem to have more restricted social lives than the older teenagers from the special school system. It seems as though it may be more difficult for them to find friends or partners, and to settle into a social network, than it is for those from special schools.

See also:
- *Social development for individuals with Down syndrome* [DSii-14-01]
- *Social development for children with Down syndrome (11-16 years)* [DSii-14-04]

The implications of these findings are that parents need to encourage friends with and without disabilities. The implications for schools and for an effective inclusive school system which can provide academic and social advantages are discussed further on page 29.

Brothers and sisters

As has been indicated in other studies, brothers and sisters play an important part in the social lives of teenagers with Down syndrome as 83% of all the teenagers frequently join in social activities with their brothers and sisters. Only about 25% of the teenagers are reported to enjoy *any* of their social activities, without the support of a member of their family. As a consequence of limited independent travel skills, most teenagers are relatively socially isolated for their age.

Summary

In summary, the social and leisure interests of teenagers are age-appropriate, but they are relatively socially isolated compared to typically developing peers. Teenagers with Down syndrome have friends, but cannot meet up with them easily out of school, limiting the opportunities for close friendships.

The school placement of teenagers influences their opportunities for making friends with both disabled and non-disabled peers, and this may have longer term social and emotional consequences.

Achievements at 16 years

Many teenagers with Down syndrome will be on the way to complete independence in personal care, able to choose their own clothes appropriately for the day, wash and bathe with minimum help, make a simple snack, answer the telephone and help with household tasks, but some will still need support for daily activities. Many teenagers will be quite socially confident in school and at clubs and only need minimal support to function in these settings. However, some young people will still need a high level of support with their personal care and in social situations.

Many teenagers will be progressing with reading and writing, with some teenagers able to write short stories and record their work in lessons while others still need full support to do so. Some teenagers will be calculating with numbers to 1000 or beyond but some will still be learning to count with numbers to 20. Teenagers will be progressing with their understanding of time and money at varying rates. It is possible for teenagers to benefit from access to the full school curriculum, differentiated to their needs, whatever their rate of progress, provided that there is adequate support in schools for this to be achieved.

Most teenagers will be enjoying music, dance, drama, art and sporting activities and developing their skills at varying rates. In these activities, the enthusiasm and creativity of teachers will have considerable influence on the way in which teenagers with Down syndrome progress. Participation in these activities is not dependent on good speech and language skills and individuals with Down syndrome can often show considerable talent if given the opportunity. Mime and dance activities, for example, allow teenagers to express their understanding of emotions and behaviour in a way they cannot do in daily life.

Most teenagers with Down syndrome can behave in an age-appropriate and socially acceptable manner, at home, at school and in the community, regardless of their level of ability, if they are expected to do so. This is a very important goal, as behaviour influences all aspects of teenagers' lives, and the lives of their families. During teenage years, difficult behaviour causes stress in the family and reduces teenagers' learning and social opportunities. In adult life, a person who can behave in a socially acceptable manner can participate fully in community and social activities. In the authors' experience, less cognitively able adults with good social behaviour will be working and leading more fulfilling lives than more cognitively able individuals with poor social behaviour.

Social independence

Independence in the community will vary. Teenagers with Down syndrome who have been educated in fairly large mainstream schools will have had the opportunity to learn to find their way around a large site, to use the canteen for lunch (involving choices and the use of money) and they may be walking to school with friends, crossing roads or using the bus. Teenagers in special education may be part of much smaller communities (50 to 70 pupils rather than 1000-1500 pupils), with less opportunity to achieve these levels of independence. Out of school, teenager's opportunities will vary according to the resources of the areas in which they live. Some teenagers may walk to a local shop or club if they are very close to home, by the time they are 11 years old, but most children with Down syndrome will become more independent in their communities during their teenage years. Most teenagers in the 11 to 16 age range will still be supervised when they travel outside the home, but they should be learning to walk to local shops and to cross roads safely.

Individual differences

For all teenagers, including those with Down syndrome, developmental progress at any age is influenced by their biological make-up and their opportunities to learn and develop throughout their lives. Throughout childhood, much learning is influenced by the social relationships experienced in families and by social learning and educational opportunities with other children and adults outside the family. It is also influenced by children's self-confidence and self-esteem. Brain development is a process which continues through life and brain function and structure are influenced by learning and activity.

Additional difficulties

It is also important to remember that a teenager with Down syndrome may have additional difficulties, like any other child. A small number of teenagers with Down syndrome have additional medical complications, like seizures or other illnesses, which may affect their development. Similarly, a small number of teenagers have autistic spectrum disorders, attention deficit or hyperactivity disorder. These additional difficulties affect less than 10% of children with Down syndrome but they should be recognised and treated in their own right when they do occur. These difficulties are discussed in a little more detail on pages 25-26.

Healthcare needs

Teenagers with Down syndrome are at greater risk for some illnesses and for hearing and visual difficulties. Any young person's developmental progress will be influenced by illness or sensory difficulties, so that it is important that all healthcare issues are understood and addressed. The second section of this module (see page 35) provides a guide to the healthcare needs of teenagers with Down syndrome, explains assessments and treatments and gives references to further reading. It is perhaps worth noting that some illnesses will present with obvious symptoms but some may not. For example, a teenager with limited language who has an ear ache or a stomach ache may not be able to explain that he or she is in pain, except by being unhappy and, maybe, irritable or difficult. Therefore it is always important to consider and rule out illness if a young person's mood changes, they stop making progress or they are difficult, before assuming they are simply being unco-operative or naughty.

Parents and teachers of typically developing teenagers have some idea about expected rates of development, which they can use to decide whether their teenagers are making appropriate progress or whether they should be worrying about their progress. For parents and teachers of young people with

Influences on development

- Social learning opportunities at home, at school and in the community
- Social support for learning through scaffolding, modelling and teaching
- Self-esteem, curiosity and motivation to learn
- Biology and experience interact to influence brain structure and brain function throughout life

An overview of the development of teenagers with Down syndrome

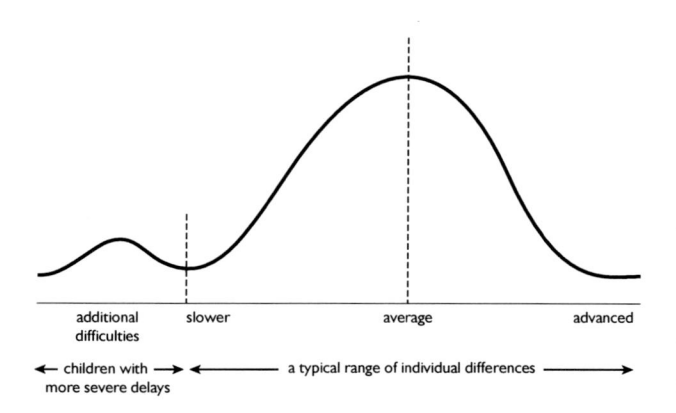

Figure 7. The spectrum of abilities in individuals with Down syndrome

Down syndrome, guidelines are equally important but more difficult to find and to interpret.

In each of the detailed modules, milestone data is included if available, for example, for speech and language, counting or reading. Young people with Down syndrome vary widely in their rates of progress. Some young people make much slower progress than others and it is not possible to predict or explain these differences fully at the present time.

Typically developing children also show a wide range of rates of progress, due to both different genetic make-ups and to social and educational learning opportunities and the range for some 85-90% of children with Down syndrome is probably due to exactly the same factors. However, as has already been identified, the development of approximately 10% to 12% of individuals with Down syndrome is being affected by additional difficulties. This group of young people show the greatest developmental delays and may be significantly more disabled as adults than the majority of individuals with Down syndrome. This is illustrated in Figure 7. The most common reasons for the more severe levels of developmental delay seem to be health issues, autism and attention deficit/hyperactivity disorder.

Teenagers with more severe developmental delays

Health problems

In both the authors' studies of teenagers with Down syndrome in 1987 and in 1999, it was clear that one reason for more severe developmental delay was additional health difficulties such as seizures and neurological damage. However, for some teenagers with severe developmental delay, the reasons cannot be identified. The prevalence of medical and psychiatric disorders in people with Down syndrome varies from those which have a lower incidence to those which are relatively common and some of these are described in the Health section of this module (see p.35).

Autism

It was once thought that Autistic Spectrum Disorders (ASD) were not found in individuals with Down syndrome. This is now known to be incorrect, but the incidence of ASD in people with Down syndrome remains a matter of some debate. It has been estimated to affect some 3-7% of children and adults. The reason for this uncertainty is that there have been no large scale controlled studies of this issue and, more importantly, that the diagnosis of ASD is too uncertain to produce reliable data.

The diagnosis of ASD is based on obtaining the developmental history of the individual and information about their behavioural patterns. At present there are no objective findings in ASD which are of diagnostic value. ASD is a spectrum disorder which covers a very wide range and there are many behavioural features which are associated with this group of conditions. However, many of these symptoms are non-specific in that they may be found in a large number of other disorders.

Some of the main characteristics of the condition are:-

See also:
- An overview of less typical developmental issues in Down syndrome [DSii-01-09]

- A lack of behaviours in which points of interest are shared with others.
- Inappropriate social behaviour which is not understood by other people.
- Abnormal interpersonal relationships, expressed as the inability to develop intimate, reciprocal communication with other people.
- Language usage which is not only delayed but abnormal in kind.
- Rigid, unimaginative style of thinking and behaviour.
- Play patterns which are repetitive, show a lack of understanding of the symbolic meaning of toys, and inability to pretend.
- Obsessional/repetitive behaviours and preoccupations.

A teenager displaying one of these characteristics, or even two or three, does not necessarily have autism. In fact, a number of these characteristics are very common in young people with Down syndrome, reflecting slow development of speech, language and play skills or differences in temperament. For a diagnosis of autism to be appropriate, a majority of these symptoms need to be present.

Attention Deficit Hyperactivity Disorder (ADHD)

This condition is sometimes confused with ASD, especially if the child has severe learning disabilities. The level of intrinsic activity and liveliness in children varies enormously and the vast majority of young people with Down syndrome are normal boisterous youngsters. However, a small number are so overactive that their entire pattern of behaviour is disorganised. They are characterised by their short attention span, impulsiveness, 'silly' social behaviour, clumsiness and constant movement which is little affected by environmental influences. The response of teenagers with ADHD to the commonly used medications is interesting because they become calmer and more capable when prescribed drugs which are pharmacological stimulants.

The management of this condition consists of a combination of behaviour modification and drugs. If parents and/or carers observe behaviours in a teenager with Down syndrome which are similar to those described above it is important to obtain a diagnostic assessment from a specialist paediatrician or a child psychiatrist with experience of young people with learning difficulties to find out if the child has additional problems.

Meeting the educational and developmental needs of teenagers with Down syndrome

During the secondary school years, teenagers with Down syndrome usually make significant progress. They will benefit from the quality of the teaching and educational environment. Recent studies indicate that the achievements of teenagers with Down syndrome have steadily improved with access to better education and changing social attitudes.[21,22] Their speech and language abilities and motor skills will be the areas of greatest delay and therefore, they will continue to benefit from speech and language therapy and from occupational and physiotherapy.

It is important that parents, teachers and therapists work together as a team if possible, with professionals recognising that the most important influences on any teenager's development come from the family and respecting the fact that parents know their teenager better than anyone else. This partnership

An overview of the development of teenagers with Down syndrome

will enable children to make optimal progress and help to support families. Later in this section, specific goals have been identified for parents and for the key professionals, reflecting their different roles and expertise. Parents tend to be very knowledgeable about Down syndrome by the time their child is eleven years old.

This section begins with an overview of the health needs of teenagers with Down syndrome and their specific profile of cognitive and developmental strengths and weaknesses, as an understanding of this profile is essential for planning effective teaching and therapy. This leads to a brief discussion of education research and goals for teachers, followed by goals for speech and language therapists, occupational therapists and physiotherapists. The final section discusses family perspectives and provides goals for families.

Health and sensory impairments

All developmental progress will be affected by illness or ongoing health problems. The common health issues for parents and teachers of teenagers to be aware of are dealt with in the Health section on page 35. It is particularly important to be alert to hearing difficulties as they affect some 50-60% of teenagers and even mild conductive losses can have a significant effect on the teenagers' development. Many teenagers (85%) also have visual impairments, and clearly any hearing and visual difficulties will influence progress in the classroom. If teenagers have hearing aids, it is important that they are properly maintained and adjusted. If teenagers have glasses, they will need to be kept clean during the day.

A specific developmental profile

Over the last 15 to 20 years, researchers have made progress in understanding the effects of having Down syndrome on development, though there is still much more to learn. Research has identified a specific profile of developmental strengths and weaknesses.[23,24] This profile is specific to children with Down syndrome, and makes their learning needs different from most other children and teenagers with similar levels of cognitive abilities. However, while this profile is typically associated with Down syndrome, the degree to which any individual with Down syndrome shows this pattern will vary. It is helpful as a guide to understanding any individual's developmental needs and learning profile. He or she may have all or none of these characteristics and if he or she does have some, the degree to which they show any strength or weakness will need to be assessed in order to develop appropriate teaching programmes and therapy.

While young people with Down syndrome experience some delays in all areas of development, the extent of the delay is not the same across all areas of development.

Social understanding and social interactive skills are a relative strength and less delayed than speech and language skills. Most teenagers are socially sensitive and understand the non-verbal cues to emotions, such as facial expression, tones of voice and body postures. Most teenagers continue to show good empathy and good understanding of social behaviours, but they will not have the language abilities to explain how they feel or to negotiate social situations.

Motor skills are delayed but the main milestones are steadily achieved and most young people become mobile and independent in self-help skills, such

An overview of the development of teenagers with Down syndrome

as feeding and dressing, which require motor skills. By secondary school age gross and fine motor skills may still be delayed. This will affect taking part in games and physical education. It will also affect handwriting. The advice of an occupational therapist will be beneficial for many teenagers. Fine and gross motor skills will steadily improve with practice, and most teenagers can use the mouse and keyboard to operate a computer at 11 years of age.

The authors encourage all parents to find activities for teenagers in the community for sports such as swimming, gymnastics, horse-riding, dancing or football. These sporting activities contribute to health and motor skills development - and a sporting skill provides teenagers and adults with increased leisure activities and social opportunities.

Speech and language skills are more delayed than the teenagers' non-verbal understanding and reasoning abilities. This is therefore a pattern of *specific* language impairment. Most teenagers with Down syndrome understand more language than they can use as a result of specific speech production difficulties. For this reason, using signs will still help some teenagers to communicate, to show their understanding and reduce their frustration, although most teenagers will use speech as their main mode of communication.

Teenagers of 11 to 16 years should be receiving regular speech and language therapy targeting phonology and articulation work as well as vocabulary and grammar development. However, learning to talk is a daily activity and is mostly learned with parents. The speech and language modules and checklists are designed to be used by parents, ideally with the support of a therapist, but on their own if necessary.

Working memory development, particularly verbal short-term memory, seems to be specifically impaired – again not progressing as fast as would be expected for non-verbal abilities – and this has had consequences for the teenagers' ability to learn a spoken language and to process information. All teaching in the classroom needs to take account of the teenagers' working memory difficulties.

Visual memory and visual processing are relative strengths, while auditory processing and auditory memory are more impaired. This means that teenagers with Down syndrome should be thought of as visual learners and all teaching supported with visual materials.

Reading ability is often a strength from as early as two years of age, perhaps because it builds on visual memory skills, and reading activities can be used to teach spoken language from this time. During the secondary school years the teaching of reading should be a daily priority, with teachers aware that reading activities can be designed to improve the teenagers' spoken language. Recent research studies have demonstrated that reading activities may be the most effective way to improve the spoken language of teenagers with Down syndrome and the most effective way to improve their working memories. [1,2,25,26]

Number seems to be relatively more difficult for teenagers with Down syndrome and their number skills are often delayed relative to reading skills. Current research indicates that for children with Down syndrome, their early number abilities keep up with their non-verbal mental abilities. Teaching materials should make maximum use of visual supports and materials such as Numicon.[27]

The specific developmental profile associated with Down syndrome

Teenagers with Down syndrome are all individuals and vary in their rates of progress - however, they tend to have a specific profile of strengths and weaknesses:

- *Social development and social learning* are strengths - teenagers enjoy and learn from social interaction with adults and peers
- *Motor development* is usually delayed and may hold back progress in self-help skills, joining in games, handling equipment and in writing, though the use of gesture to communicate is a strength
- *Speech and language development* is usually teenagers' area of most significant delay - it is more delayed than non-verbal abilities. Most teenagers understand more than they can say and signing is an important bridge to speaking. Speech intelligibility is usually a difficulty. A high incidence of hearing difficulties is contributing to speech and language delay.
- *Working memory development* is specifically delayed relative to non-verbal abilities, particularly the verbal short-term memory component - so that learning from listening is difficult for teenagers. Working memory also supports thinking, problem solving and reasoning. Visual and spatial processing and memory are relative strengths - so that teenagers learn effectively from visual information - they can be thought of as visual learners.
- *Social behaviour* - teenagers have strengths in social skills and in developing age-appropriate social behaviour, if this is encouraged and expected. However, their good social understanding and empathy leads them to pick up on non-verbal emotional cues, such as those for anxiety or disapproval, very quickly. They are therefore sensitive to failure and may use behavioural strategies to avoid difficult situations.

Social behaviour is a strength as young people with Down syndrome are less likely to develop difficult behaviours than other young people with similar levels of cognitive delay. However, young people with Down syndrome are, as a group, more likely to develop difficult behaviours than non-disabled young people of their age.

Most teenagers with Down syndrome are socially sensitive and understand the non-verbal cues to emotions, such as facial expression, tones of voice and body postures. They can behave appropriately in showing concern, or becoming upset. However, this sensitivity can also make teenagers vulnerable as they will quickly pick up on negative emotions such as anger, dislike or rejection. As they are usually not able to explain how they feel, their distress will be expressed in behaviour. Some young people with Down syndrome can be quite disruptive and difficult to manage at times, at home or at school, and they may use their understanding of people's behaviour to be unco-operative and the centre of attention. It is always possible to change behaviour and to encourage and teach age appropriate behaviour. However, it is not easy to change difficult behaviours that have become habits, and most difficult behaviours can be avoided with calm routines and good control.

In order to provide detailed overviews of the research and practical advice relevant to the development of teenagers with Down syndrome in this modular series, individual modules address social development and behaviour, and motor development, and four cognitive areas - 1) speech, language and communication, 2) reading and writing, 3) number and 4) working memory skills. This division is somewhat arbitrary and reflects the focus of the team of authors. Self-help skills are covered in social development and behaviour.

Education

It can be argued that the most important influence on a young person's progress between 11 and 16 years is their school experience and this is equally true for young people with Down syndrome. Finding the right secondary school place will usually be more difficult for parents of a teenager with Down syndrome than for parents of typically developing children.

Inclusive or special education

The significant benefits of inclusive schooling have been mentioned earlier in this module. The available studies all indicate very significant positive effects of inclusion in school on the spoken language development of children and teenagers and on their academic progress, particularly for reading, writing and arithmetic.[1,2,28,29] The personal independence, social independence and behaviour of the included teenagers have been reported to be either the same or better when compared with equally able peers in special education settings. These benefits result from being immersed in the typical social world and the normal spoken language world of the mainstream school as well as the increased support for learning, and access to the same curriculum as the other children. The authors and their colleagues have been directly involved in the support of children and teenagers with Down syndrome in mainstream schools for the past 13 years and they believe that the level of daily support for reading and writing and the access to the full curriculum, alongside non-disabled peers in the classroom, has played a significant part in the speech and language progress of these young people. It is not possible to create the same learning environment in a special class or special

> **Education for teenagers with Down syndrome**
>
> - all teachers need to know about the specific cognitive profile associated with Down syndrome, and adapt their teaching appropriately
> - inclusive education leads to very significant gains in spoken language abilities
> - inclusive education leads to equally significant gains in reading, writing and arithmetic
> - personal independence skills and behaviour progress similarly in special or inclusive education
> - the development of friendship skills needs further research, especially for teenagers, who may lose out on close and mutual friendships in inclusive settings

school, however dedicated the teachers. The typically developing peer group is essential for an optimum educational environment.

At present, the social aspects of inclusion in the UK are not as good as they could be in two ways. Firstly, schools are not yet as confident in promoting social inclusion as they are in providing good access to the curriculum. Many schools have yet to recognise that the main resource that they have to support the social inclusion of pupils with disabilities is all the other pupils in school. The peer group could usually be much more actively involved in supporting teenagers with Down syndrome, but this requires planning and support.[45-48] All pupils need to have the opportunity to discuss disability issues and to be actively supported in learning how to support pupils with significant disabilities. North American schools tend to be further advanced on this front and therefore children with disabilities are more fully part of the school and the home communities.

Secondly, the teenager with a specific or significant disability may not have the benefit of a peer group of disabled teenagers, and, in the authors' view this peer group is important. It is good to have some opportunities to engage in activities with friends on the basis of equality of skills and understanding. Friendships with non-disabled peers are not quite the same and are often 'helping' in nature rather than fun and mutually supportive relationships. Identity issues become important in adolescence. Successful adult adjustment, for everyone, requires a realistic appraisal of who we are and our strengths and weaknesses. It is important for teenagers with disabilities to have friends with similar disabilities for mutual support and understanding. It is good to know that you are not the only one facing the world with your particular difficulties. It is important to know adults with similar disabilities to provide positive support and realistic role models for adult life. It is also important to be able to form close and mutually supportive friendships and partnerships and successful ones are usually based on similar abilities and interests.

These peer group issues would not exist in a fully inclusive school system, with all teenagers with moderate or severe learning difficulties in neighbourhood schools, but at present, in the UK and in other countries, many teenagers with Down syndrome are likely to be included in mainstream schools while their learning disabled peer group are still in segregated schools or classes. Given the recorded benefits of inclusive education, everyone interested in the welfare of teenagers with Down syndrome should be working towards ensuring that school systems become fully inclusive.

Choosing a mainstream secondary placement will not be straightforward, as parents often have to battle for a place and then may be faced with a secondary school situation where the teachers are not confident about meeting their young person's needs. There is still much education and training needed in most countries if teachers are to feel well equipped to teach in fully inclusive school systems. Parents of a teenager in a mainstream placement will also find that they have to be more involved and take more responsibility for supporting the education of their teenager, going to regular meetings and working closely with the teachers and Learning Support Assistants. Teachers in mainstream schools will find that they need to develop a close partnership with parents when teaching a teenager with a disability such as Down syndrome.

See also:
- *Education for individuals with Down syndrome - an overview* [DSii-16-01]
- *Education for individuals with Down syndrome - whole school issues* [DSii-16-05]

See also:
- *Accessing the curriculum - Strategies for differentiation for pupils with Down syndrome* [DSii-16-07]

Meeting the specific educational needs associated with Down syndrome in special or mainstream classes

The educational needs of teenagers with Down syndrome are the same whether they are in mainstream or special classes. Their special educational needs should be met, taking account of priorities and adaptations to teaching methods in all classrooms. The key goals are set out in the list below and developed more fully in the specific topic modules for this age range.

Goals for teachers of 11-16 year olds with Down syndrome

- to involve the teenager in all aspects of school life and school routines
- to support social independence in school and the development of friendships with peers
- to support the development of leisure skills and inclusion with peers in break and lunchtimes
- to encourage, model and expect age-appropriate, socially acceptable behaviour at all times
- to be familiar with the research findings which demonstrate a specific cognitive profile associated with Down syndrome (see pages 16-17) and to adapt teaching methods appropriately
- to provide access to all areas of the school curriculum at a level appropriate for the individual teenager
- to recognise the importance of teaching reading and writing daily, to develop speech, language and working memory skills as well as literacy skills
- to have clear targets for speech and language work for each teenager, and identify how these can be absorbed into all aspects of the curriculum
- to facilitate independent learning and the ability to work and to learn as part of a group
- to make full use of computer aided learning, with appropriate software for individual and group work

Speech and language therapy

At eleven years of age, most young people with Down syndrome are able to use speech as their main form of communication and they should be encouraged to do so. The use of sign as a support will still be valuable but parents and teachers should be aware that sign can be used as a prompt for new words and to aid short-term memory but the focus must be on helping the teenager to develop clear spoken language. Too much use of signing in an unplanned way may actually delay the development of clear spoken language at this stage.

Most eleven year olds will be using 2 to 3 keywords joined together or short sentences in their spoken communication, while understanding more vocabulary and grammar than this would indicate. Many teenagers will still be difficult to understand and need help with developing clear speech. Ideally all teenagers with Down syndrome should receive speech and language therapy but access to this service will vary considerably from place to place. There is a large research literature documenting the specific speech and language profile of young people with Down syndrome and identifying their needs. There is also universal agreement among international experts on the speech and language therapy needs of teenagers with Down syndrome. However, this information does not yet inform the provision of services everywhere and there is a need to encourage specialist training for speech and language therapist who work with teenagers with Down syndrome.

Goals for speech and language therapists working with 11-16 year olds with Down syndrome

- to have up-to-date knowledge of the specific research literature on speech and language development, working memory and effective therapies for teenagers with Down syndrome
- to understand the significance of the specific impairment in the phonological loop component of working memory for the speech and language profile associated with Down syndrome
- to understand the importance of reading work to support the development of vocabulary, grammar and speech clarity, using strengths in visual memory
- to understand the importance of auditory discrimination for speech sounds, phonics activities, phonological awareness training and speech work for improving working memory function
- to have clear targets for 4 areas of work, speech, vocabulary, grammar and communication skills and to keep detailed records of progress
- for vocabulary and grammar, to have separate targets for comprehension and for production, as comprehension in both domains is typically significantly ahead of production
- for speech work, separate targets may be needed for articulation, phonology and intelligibility (pacing, voice etc)
- to review oral-motor function, feeding, chewing and drinking patterns and advise accordingly
- all targets should be shared with parents, teachers and assistants
- teenagers with Down syndrome should be seen at least monthly in school, targets reviewed and activities set for parents, teachers and assistants to include in their daily routines
- these activities should be modelled with the teenager by the speech and language therapist, if parents and assistants are expected to deliver therapy
- ideally, all teenagers with Down syndrome of secondary school age should have weekly individual or group sessions of speech and language therapy with a therapist who has specialist knowledge and the skills to address their profile of difficulties, particularly for speech and intelligibility work.

Reviews of the literature supporting these recommended goals[12,13,14] and specialised workshops[49] are available for speech and language therapists. Specialised accredited postgraduate training is being developed at the University of Portsmouth for speech and language therapists and for teachers to begin in autumn 2002.

Motor skills

While almost all teenagers with Down syndrome will be walking, running and be reasonably mobile by eleven years of age, most will still show some delay in the control of gross motor skills and will have more difficulty writing, drawing and painting than other teenagers. They may benefit from the advice of an expert and this may be an occupational therapist, a physiotherapist or a specialist teacher for young people with motor delays and difficulties.

Goals for occupational therapists and physiotherapists

- to provide programmes of activity to develop gross motor skills and spatial awareness
- to advise on adaptations and specific activities to enable teenagers to participate in the school PE and games curriculum
- to advise parents on suitable sporting, dance or gymnastics activities and any adaptations necessary to enable their teenager to participate
- to advise teachers and parents on suitable seating and posture in the classroom and at home
- to provide activities and adaptations to develop fine motor skills, fine motor co-ordination and handwriting
- to review progress with independent drinking, feeding, toileting and dressing, if necessary, and advise on any adaptations needed

Family issues

See also:
- *Issues for families with children with Down syndrome* [DSii-18-01]

There is now a growing body of research on the life of families with a member who has Down syndrome and this work is reviewed in detail in the module on the family. The research studies are largely reassuring,[20,30,31] as they show that most families find the resources to cope with the special needs of the young person with Down syndrome and still lead ordinary family lives. There is no evidence that brothers and sisters are negatively affected in the majority of families or that more marriages break down. This does not mean that there are not times of stress or difficulty, but most people do cope.

It helps to have friends, family and neighbours for emotional and practical help at times, so it is advantageous for parents to avoid social isolation. Many families report that they have found the support of other families with teenagers with Down syndrome invaluable also, and that parent groups are a source of emotional and practical help. It also helps to have up-to-date and accurate information on the needs of teenagers and on the services available in the local community.

The available evidence on outcomes in adult life indicates that the most important developmental and learning experiences for a young person with Down syndrome will come from being the much loved member of a happy, active family - and from doing all the things that the family does. It is, therefore, very important that parents recognise this and take care to balance the additional needs of the young person with Down syndrome with the needs of themselves and the rest of the family.

Goals for parents of 11-16 year olds with Down syndrome

- to fully involve teenagers in family life
- to involve teenagers in a range of social activities in the community with typically developing peers and disabled peers
- to involve teenagers in sporting activities to develop fitness, and leisure skills for sustaining teenage and adult inclusion
- to provide a stimulating speech and language environment by ensuring that teenagers are listened to and fully involved in family talk
- to require socially acceptable and age-appropriate behaviour at home and in all social activities
- to plan, with help if necessary, to change any difficult behaviours that have developed
- to steadily encourage independence in personal care and in the community
- to encourage the further development of reading, writing, number and money skills in partnership with secondary school

In summary

In order to meet the developmental and educational needs of teenagers with Down syndrome during their secondary school years, it is important to take account of their health, social and behavioural development, their speech, language and communication needs, their educational needs and their motor skill development. In an ideal situation, this will happen as the result of parents, physicians, speech and language therapists, teachers and physical therapists sharing their knowledge and expertise and working together as a team. Many of the goals for teenagers with Down syndrome should be age-appropriate, recognising that the teenagers will move through life stages on the basis of chronological age and that successful inclusion in schools, communities and families, requires age-appropriate social behaviour.

Everyone involved with teenagers with Down syndrome should have some understanding of their specific profile of strengths and weaknesses and understand the central importance of addressing their speech, language and working memory difficulties in order to advance their cognitive development. They should also be aware of the research evidence which indicates that daily involvement in reading instruction is one of the most effective ways of improving speech, language and working memory skills.

Education in fully inclusive school systems leads to significant gains in spoken language and academic skills, which will enhance the work opportunities and quality of life for teenagers when they reach adulthood. Teenagers with Down syndrome should have the opportunity to have friends with Down syndrome and with other learning disabilities as well as being fully included by peers without disabilities, for the development of a positive self-identity and the opportunity to have close, reciprocal friendships based on mutual understanding and on similar abilities and interests.

Everyone involved with teenagers needs to have a vision of preparing them for a normal adult life, as most will achieve a high degree of personal independence, autonomy and normality if encouraged to do so.

II. Health care for teenagers with Down syndrome

Teenagers with Down syndrome, like typically developing teenagers, may be affected by any type of illness. However, it is recommended that all teenagers and adults with Down syndrome have regular health checks to detect certain disorders as soon as possible. These systematic health checks should be carried out because people with Down syndrome tend to be affected by a number of disorders more commonly than other people.

Some of the health issues which are of particular importance for teenagers with Down syndrome are the same as those for younger children (hearing, vision, thyroid, sleep apnoeas, atlanto-axial instability), others seem to fall in incidence (behavioural sleep difficulties, infections) and there are some new concerns for this age group (dental issues, puberty and sexual health, obesity and mental health).

In the authors' recent survey of 46 teenagers aged 11 to 20 years, 14 (30%) were on regular medications, 7 for thyroid, 3 for asthma, 1 for possible epilepsy manifested as unusual aggressive outbursts, 1 for depression, 1 for colitis and 1 for overactivity.[1,2]

Other medical problems reported were 2 cases of kidney/bladder problems, 2 cases of scoliosis of the spine, 1 case of Perthes disease, 1 of leukaemia but now in remission, 1 of 'slight' atlanto-axial instability, 1 case of sleep apnoea, 1 case of eye infections, 1 case of persistent constipation, 2 cases of problems with teeth and 1 of 'scaly' scalp. Hearing losses were reported for 18 (39%) of the teenagers and 39 (85%) had visual defects, with 34 wearing glasses. Parents considered that 22 (48%) of the teenagers were overweight. Two of the 5 most developmentally delayed teenagers were described as autistic.

Of those disorders which have a higher prevalence in people with Down syndrome there are several which are of particular importance because they are relatively easy to diagnose and treat, because they are preventable or because they may have a high popular profile. These disorders and the health issues relevant to adolescence are included in this section.

These disorders and issues are as follows:-

- Disorders of hearing
- Disorders of vision
- Infections
- Disorders of thyroid function
- Constipation and diarrhoea
- Congenital disorders of the heart
- Atlanto-axial instability
- Sleep disturbances and sleep apnoea
- Obesity and healthy eating
- Dental care
- Puberty and sexual health
- Mental health

These disorders and their treatments are explained in this health section.

Hearing disorders

Children with Down syndrome tend to have a significantly higher incidence of hearing problems than other groups and almost all surveys conclude that about 80% of them will have some problem with hearing.[32] Studies of teenagers suggest that the incidence is lower (50-60%) but this is still a much higher incidence than would be found in the general population. One Canadian study reported that in a group of 34 teenagers with Down syndrome, 20 (59%) of the teenagers had hearing loss in at least one ear and 41% had losses in both ears.[33] Of the teenagers with hearing loss, 6 had wax blocking the ear canal and causing deafness, identifying the need for good hygiene and regular checking for dry wax. Ten of the teenagers had sensori-neural loss, 5 had conductive loss and 5 had both types of loss.

A study from the USA[34] reports similar figures for 18-20 year olds with Down syndrome, with some 48% with no hearing loss, some 13% had conductive losses, 13% sensorineural and 26% mixed losses. Some 40% of the teenagers had abnormal tympanograms, due to the long-term damaging effect of 'glue ear' in infants and young children. The incidence of hearing loss in this group of young adults with Down syndrome was much greater than in a comparison group of young adults with learning disabilities but not Down syndrome, 80% of whom had normal hearing. In this study, individuals with hearing losses performed less well on speech and language tasks and speech discrimination tasks.

In the authors' recent survey of 46 teenagers in the UK, 18 (39%) were reported to have hearing loss, 7 having moderate to severe losses and 11 having mild losses. Seven teenagers were using binaural (two) hearing aids. The teenagers with hearing losses were all having regular checks, with all having had a test within the previous 18 months and most having annual checks. Of the 28 reported to have no hearing loss, 23 could not report the last time they had had a hearing assessment. As other studies indicate a 50% incidence of hearing loss at this age, it is likely that some 4 or 5 teenagers in this study had undetected hearing loss. Of the 22 teenagers receiving regular hearing assessments, 4 were being seen at their schools and the rest at a hospital clinic.

There is some evidence of sensori-neural hearing losses increasing with age for individuals with Down syndrome and therefore it is important to continue with hearing checks at least every 3 years. (Some readers may be interested to note that in a similar survey in 1987, 80% of parents could not remember when their son or daughter had last had a hearing test and only 12% of the group were known to have hearing losses suggesting that many of those young people had undetected losses. Clearly, audiological care in the UK has improved significantly).

The importance of hearing cannot be overemphasised. The vast majority of teenagers with Down syndrome are still acquiring language and good hearing is involved in the continued development of speech and language as well as in socialisation. These, as well as other factors, have a profound effect upon the general intellectual development of the young person. The detection and continued treatment of hearing difficulties will be of great benefit to the teenager with Down syndrome.

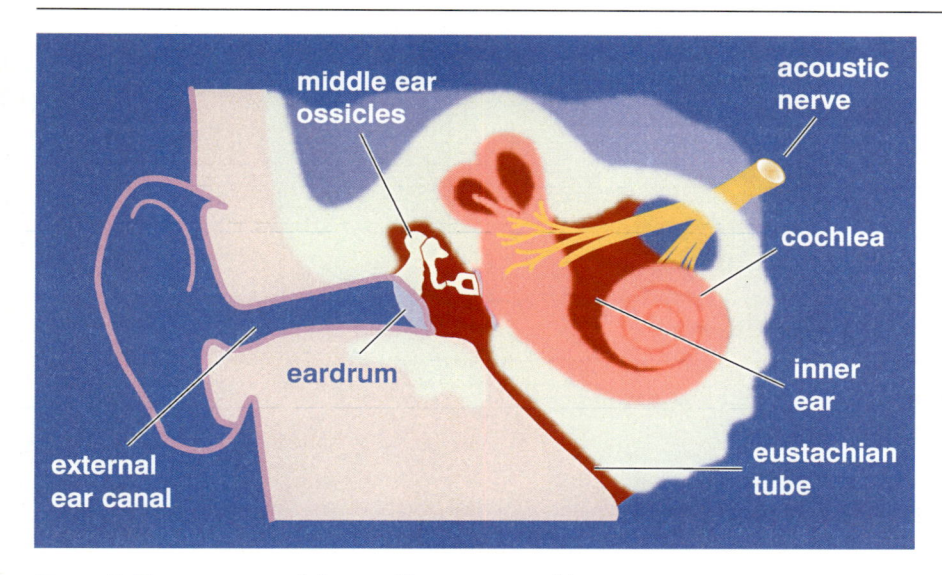

Figure 8. The structure of the ear (diagram - not to scale)

Hearing and the function of the ear

Sounds, which are pressure waves in the air, travel along the *external auditory canal* and impinge upon the *eardrum*. This causes the eardrum to vibrate which, in turn, produces movements in the bones or *ossicles* in the *middle ear*. These movements produce vibrations upon the *oval window* (a small membrane separating the middle ear from the inner ear) and, via the fluid in the *inner ear*, stimulate the *hair cells* of the *cochlea* differentially, depending upon their various frequencies and pressures. It is at this stage that the information that is contained in these pressure changes is transformed (transduced) into nerve impulses which travel along the *acoustic nerve* via complex routes to the brainstem and brain where sound is perceived. Anything which interferes with any stage of this transfer chain will affect hearing.

The detection and diagnosis of hearing problems depends largely upon two factors:-

(1) the routine screening of all young children as part of the prevailing public health program

(2) the existence of a high level of suspicion on the part of carers that a hearing problem might be present.

Because of the high incidence of hearing problems in children with Down syndrome, and the fact that special testing techniques are sometimes needed, it is recommended that all of them should undergo appropriate hearing tests in a properly equipped and staffed audiology centre. The choice of which tests to use will depend upon circumstances and expert advice should be sought about this. The following descriptions are only a very short introduction to the subject.

Tympanometry (or impedance or compliance testing) is a commonly used test that records the manner in which the ear drum moves under test conditions and this provides information about the function of the middle ear. It is a painless test but it does require a degree of co-operation from the child.

In the UK it is Government policy for all children to have their hearing evaluated shortly after birth with the *Oto Acoustic Emission Test (OAE)*. This test is purely passive in that it does not require any active participation from the child and is, therefore, suitable for very young children. There are several versions of this test but they are all based on the detection and analysis of certain sounds which are *produced* by the inner ear. OAE is mainly useful for the detection of sensori-neural deafness, and other passive tests, which measure the way in which the eardrum moves, are used to detect middle ear problems.

Visual Response Audiometry, VRA, is now being used for older children. This test is one of a group of *behavioural* tests in which the child is *conditioned* to respond to sounds and is, therefore, useful for children who cannot be relied on to actively cooperate in responding to different types of sounds.

Where children are able to understand instructions to respond when they hear a sound, *pure tone audiometry* may be used. There are a number of versions of this technique, the principle of which is to test hearing by producing tones of known loudness and pitch in small increments. The child signals whenever he hears a specific tone and the responses are plotted on a chart – the *audiogram*.

The audiogram covers the range of frequencies (pitch) from 125 to 8000 Hz (cycles per second), and the range of loudness from zero to 100 dB (decibels).

The decibel is the standard unit of measurement for the *intensity* of sound, and is recorded on a logarithmic scale on the audiogram, separately for each ear.

A person with normal hearing will have a line from the lowest frequency tested, 125 Hz (cycles per second), to the highest frequency tested, 8000 Hz, at the level of about zero decibels (see Figure 9).

Figure 10 shows the audiogram from one ear of a person with a conductive hearing loss of about 35 dB.

The common causes of hearing difficulties in Down syndrome are:- wax in the external ear canal, 'glue ear', infection of the middle ear (otitis media) and sensori-neural hearing loss.

Wax in the external ear canal, particularly if it is old and hard, may interfere with hearing and should always be removed. Wax-softening eardrops should be tried in the first instance but if this procedure is not successful the wax will have to be removed by syringing or with the use of an appropriate instrument. These procedures should be performed by experienced professionals since the external ear canal is usually narrower in individuals with Down syndrome and this may make the procedure more difficult to do.

Glue Ear is one of the commonest conditions involving the ear and it has a particularly high incidence in children with Down syndrome, causing conductive hearing loss. In this condition a mucoid secretion accumulates in the middle ear and has the effect of reducing hearing levels. The situation for children with Down syndrome is different because the 'glue' is stickier, is less likely to drain away, and is more likely to become infected. The Eustachian tubes, which connect the middle ear to the upper part of the throat, are often not effective in allowing drainage from the middle ear.

There are three main techniques which are used in the treatment of glue ear.

The insertion of *grommets* in the ear drum allows the fluid to drain out of the middle ear into the external auditory canal. Grommets are tiny tubes with flanges at each end which are inserted through the eardrum and allow

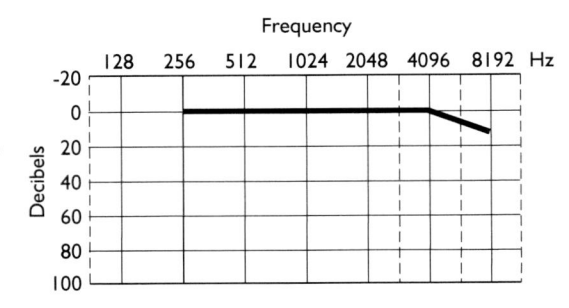

Figure 9. Normal right ear audiogram

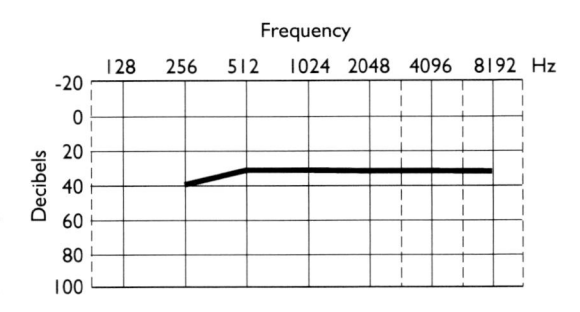

Figure 10. Conductive hearing loss

An overview of the development of teenagers with Down syndrome

the glue to drain out. Tonsillectomy and/or adenoidectomy may also be helpful. This form of treatment is effective as long as the grommets remain in position in the eardrum. They have a tendency to become extruded (pushed out), remaining in place for about three to twelve months, but they are almost always helpful in allowing drainage and therefore improving hearing.

The disadvantages of extrusion can be avoided by creating an artificial perforation in the eardrum with a laser apparatus. These laser-produced perforations tend to heal within a few weeks but many clinicians feel that the procedure is very worthwhile.

Microsuction is a technique in which the fluid in the middle ear is sucked out through a thin needle inserted through the eardrum. This procedure usually has to be repeated several times but can be very effective. It has the advantage that there is no discharge into the external auditory canal to be dealt with.

The likelihood of **Middle Ear Infections** in children with Down syndrome is considerably greater than in any comparable group of children. The reasons for this are the special problems of glue ear and the fact that individuals with Down syndrome are more susceptible to infections of all kinds. The treatment of middle ear infections usually involves the use of antibiotics and may also necessitate one of the interventions listed above for glue ear.

There is a view among some otologists that grommets should not be used because of the narrow external auditory canal found in children with Down syndrome, because they are often extruded and because continual replacement may scar the ear drum. The authors, and others,[32] disagree with this view because they feel that the benefits of improved hearing upon language development and upon socialisation as well as on general intellectual development and self-confidence outweigh the possible difficulties associated with grommets. If grommets are not appropriate for a particular child, hearing aids may be offered for conductive loss.

Sensori-neural hearing loss is a poorly understood set of conditions in which the inner ear or cochlea malfunctions. The phrase is sometimes used to include problems in other parts of the central nervous system as well. It may be constitutional or develop in later life and the higher tones are mostly affected. This type of hearing loss may have a serious effect on understanding since it is these frequencies which give speech most of its intelligibility. This type of hearing loss is often overlooked in the early stages because these children do not always behave as if they are deaf. They respond to sounds of many different kinds but what they hear is a type of low frequency rumble containing little real information. Those who can lipread may sometimes be able to communicate to some extent.

There is no cure in this group of conditions and those who benefit from the use of hearing aids continue to depend on them indefinitely.

The suggested program for routine audiology is firstly at about nine months of age and annually until ten

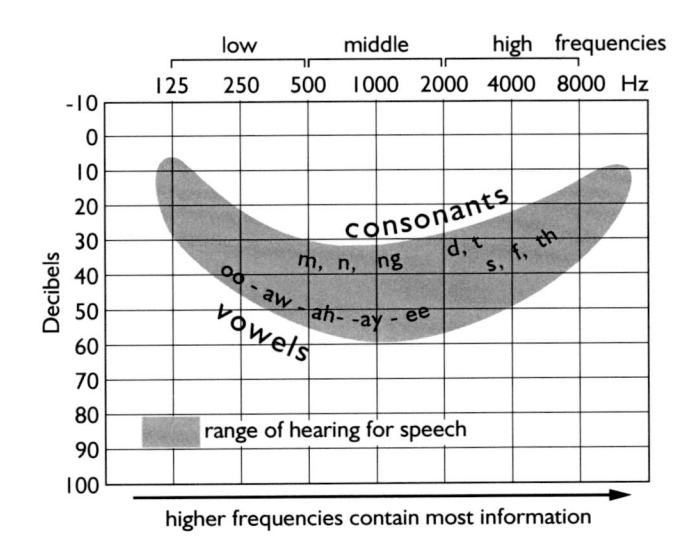

Figure II. Hearing ranges for speech sounds

years of age. After the age of ten years testing every two years is considered sufficient.

There are a number of sophisticated techniques available which test different aspects of the hearing system but it is important to remember that the only way to be sure that a child has proper sound perception is by their behavioural response to purely aural information.

Hearing Aids may be needed in a proportion of people with Down syndrome and the situation has now improved in that hearing aids are now very much more sophisticated than they used to be.

The enormous processing power of digital chips is now being used in hearing aids so that the specific requirements of children with different types of hearing loss can be compensated for much more accurately.

Getting used to wearing an aid may be a difficult problem in some cases. Children need to learn that the aid is actually helpful and a period of training may be necessary. This is often best started in a quiet room with no distracting noises so that the child can appreciate the improvement in the understanding of speech. They may then be gradually introduced into more open environments. In more difficult cases a radio-link may be helpful. This consists of a combined aid and radio receiver for the child and a transmitter-microphone for the carer. This apparatus almost totally excludes extraneous noise and allows the child to appreciate the use of aiding more easily. It is obviously very important not to give up in the face of difficulties, but to be persistent in attaining success.

Although hearing losses of up to 25 dB are usually not considered to be serious in typically developing children, there is evidence to suggest that even mild hearing loss has a deleterious effect on the educational, emotional and language development in children who have other difficulties.[see 18]

These data lend powerful support to the view that mild hearing loss is likely to have an even greater effect on children with Down syndrome.

Signing is almost always helpful in the particular situation where language development is being impeded by hearing difficulties. The advantage of this strategy is that language development can progress even in the presence of hearing difficulties.

Disorders of vision

There are a number of eye disorders which are of special relevance in Down syndrome but, apart from infections of the eyelid and conjunctiva, the commonest and most important are disorders which distort the image upon the retina. The majority of these are errors of refraction, i.e. short and long sightedness and astigmatism.

Because these errors of refraction are so common in individuals with Down syndrome it is important to have *a high index of suspicion* that they may be present. It appears that children and teenagers with Down syndrome rely on visual information to a relatively larger extent than other children. If this is so it means that vision is, relatively, even more important than it would normally be.

In the authors' survey,[1,2] parents reported that 39 of the 46 teenagers (85%) had visual defects and 38 of these young people were wearing glasses. Of the teenagers with vision defects, all had had an assessment within the last 18 months and all but 2 within the past 12 months. The majority were being seen by their own opticians, with 3 being seen at a hospital clinic. Of the 6 teenagers reported to have no vision problems, 4 parents could not recall the last time that their son or daughter had had an eye test. In 1987 54% of teenagers were reported to have vision defects and all but two of this group wore glasses, suggesting that there were undetected visual defects for about a third of that group and that eye care has improved for teenagers with Down syndrome in the UK.

Testing of visual function should be carried out routinely every year in all children with Down syndrome until the age of ten years, every two years during teenage and adult years and as soon as possible if there is any clue in the behaviour of the child or young person which could be accounted for by deteriorating vision. It is possible to test vision in virtually all children and young people, even those who are very young and/or who cannot speak.

Fortunately almost all errors of refraction are treatable with the use of spectacles. New developments in lens manufacture have made lightweight plastic lenses available, and for those whose who have a very flat nasal bridge, double bridge pieces can be very helpful. Elasticised bands which attach to the ear pieces, such as are used by sportsmen can be useful in preventing spectacles from falling off. It is important that glasses be kept clean at all times, so that the child is always aware that they really do make the world around them easier to see.

A spare pair of glasses should always be available – it is not worth the disruption of waiting for new pair if the current one is lost or damaged.

The employment of behavioural techniques may be necessary if the child refuses to wear the spectacles. In any event it is useful to create situations where the child realises that vision is improved with use of spectacles.

Disorders of thyroid function

The thyroid gland is a shield-shaped gland situated at the base of the neck. It produces three main hormones; thyroxine, triiodothyronine and calcitonin. Disorders of thyroid function (excluding calcitonin, which will not be dealt with here) are amongst the commonest of all endocrine disorders. In the United Kingdom as a whole the prevalence of hypothyroidism is 1.4% in females and 0.1% in males. The prevalence in individuals with Down syndrome, however, is considerably higher. For example, in the authors' recent survey of 46 teenagers in the UK, 9 teenagers (20%) had a thyroid problem, with 7 having hypothyroidism (underactive thyroid) and 2 having hyperthyroidism (overactive thyroid).[1,2]

Thyroxine (T4) and triiodothyronine (T3) control many aspects of development and metabolism and are essential for proper development and function.

Of the many types of thyroid disorder which may occur, much the most frequent is hypothyroidism - underactivity of thyroid function - and the prevalence of this condition in people with Down syndrome is considerably higher than in the population as a whole.

The main clinical features of hypothyroidism (under-functioning of the thyroid gland), are slowness, both physical and mental, dry hair, thickening of the skin, deepening of the voice and weight gain. In addition the following symptoms are also found; intolerance of cold, slow pulse, constipation, slowed growth velocity, deteriorating performance at school, delayed or absent puberty, and a large variety of mental problems.

These signs and symptoms vary a great deal between individuals both in degree and in the particular combinations expressed. The situation is complicated by the fact that the signs of hypothyroidism, which are often insidious in their onset, are frequently attributed to Down syndrome itself.

The clinical features of hypothyroidism on their own are not sufficient to make the diagnosis; this can only be made with certainty by the laboratory measurement of thyroid stimulating hormone (TSH) and the thyroid hormones.

TSH is a hormone which is produced by the pituitary gland and which stimulates the thyroid gland to produce T4 and T3. This hormone is usually used as an index of thyroid function because its concentration increases when the level of T4 and T3 falls. However, because the level of TSH may be sometimes higher than normal in the presence of normal thyroid function in people with Down syndrome, it is considered advisable to measure T4, T3 as well as TSH whenever thyroid function tests (TFTs) are performed. Because of the great importance of not missing a diagnosis of hypothyroidism all screening protocols advise performing TFTs periodically throughout life. The recommended intervals vary from once every five years to annual testing, the most popular suggestion being two-yearly testing. Even if the symptoms of a disorder can be explained in other ways, it is still useful to perform TFTs as part of the general investigation of most problems because of its relative commonness and the possibility of multiple diagnosis.

Treatment

Once the diagnosis of hypothyroidism has been made, the treatment consists of the administration of tablets containing T4 by mouth. The thyroxine contained in these tablets is identical to the thyroxine produced by the human thyroid gland and if the dosage is properly monitored should not produce problems.

After the initiation of treatment, follow-up visits should be held at three-monthly intervals until the appropriate dose has been established and every six to twelve months thereafter. Growth and weight should be measured at regular intervals and some estimate of cognitive progress made. It is also useful to try to obtain some idea of the general state of well being of the patient.

As children grow and their body weight increases the need for T4 will increase and it will be necessary to adjust the dose guided by the results of the TFTs.

Rarely it is found that the treatment is stopped, either because it is felt that the patient is 'cured' or for other reasons. It is, therefore, important to impress upon all those involved that the treatment of hypothyroidism is life-long, that proper monitoring is necessary and supplies of T4 are always kept available.

The treatment of hypothyroidism is not difficult, is cheap, has no side effects and, because it is perfect replacement therapy, produces ideal results.

An overview of the development of teenagers with Down syndrome

Infection in people with Down syndrome

The increased incidence of infections in people with Down syndrome is very well documented. Until the nineteen fifties it was the leading case of morbidity and mortality in Down syndrome.

Respiratory infections are particularly common, especially during the first five years of life, and infections of the skin and the bladder are also common.

The great increase in longevity in people with Down syndrome is primarily due to modern methods of treating infection. There is evidence that people with Down syndrome have this increased susceptibility to infection because their immune systems have some abnormalities. Fortunately this does not mean that they do not respond to immunisation procedures or antibiotics, but it does mean that they are prone to more frequent infections than control groups and that they are sometimes more difficult to treat.

The implications of this increased susceptibility is that antibiotics tend to be needed more frequently in people with Down syndrome and it is likely that they will need to be used earlier in the course of an infection as well.

Immunisations ought to be carried out in the normal way but it is sometimes necessary to ensure that the antibody response is adequate. Immunisation against hepatitis B is now commonly included with the usual list of childhood immunisations since the incidence seems to be higher in people with Down syndrome. This disease is highly infectious and a good case could be made for everyone to be immunised against it.

The presence of *occult*, or hidden infections should be suspected if a child with Down syndrome seems below par for no obvious reason. Common sites for such infections are in the bladder, the throat and tonsils, the teeth, the middle ear and the skin.

Generally, problems with infections tend to decrease as the person with Down syndrome grows older.

Table 1 shows the percentage of teenagers who suffered from infections often, and the common types of infections reported in the authors' 1987 and 1999 surveys in the UK.

The figures indicate that there has been little change in infection rates over the 12 year period. Coughs and colds seem a little more prevalent for the teenagers attending mainstream schools and stomach and skin infections more common for those attending special schools. Skin infections can become more troublesome during adolescence and good hygiene needs to be encouraged plus the use of antiseptic ointments for septic spots.

Gastro-intestinal system

People with Down syndrome are more likely to have more problems with the stomach and intestines than other comparable groups of people. One

Table 1. Frequency of Common Illnesses

Question	Mainstream '99 (%)	Special '99 (%)	'87 Data (%)
Often suffers from coughs	27	16	21
Often suffers from colds	42	18	30
Often suffers from sore throats	0	12	9
Often suffers from ear infections	0	13	8
Often suffers from skin infections	17	31	20
Often suffers from stomach upsets	0	26	13

of the commonest of these is constipation. If the constipation is very serious the child should, preferably, be investigated by a paediatric gastroenterologist since there are some rather serious conditions of the gut which present in this way. If special investigations reveal no obvious reason for the constipation it may then be managed symptomatically.

Occasionally the lower part of the colon becomes greatly distended and chronically filled with faeces. This can be a difficult problem to deal with and emptying the lower colon can be difficult. The help of a physician experienced in techniques for emptying the colon may be needed.

Even if the child has a good mixed diet and has an adequate fluid intake, constipation may continue to be a problem and the management then usually consists of a combination of habit training and laxatives.

The use of laxatives should be closely monitored as to dosage and frequency since these details often determine the difference between success and failure. It seems that constipation problems do tend to resolve as children get older as only one teenager in the authors' survey group of 46 teenagers still suffered from constipation.

Cardio-vascular system

Although incidence figures vary, it is generally accepted that about 50% of babies born with Down syndrome will have a disorder of the heart. These congenital cardiac disorders vary enormously in type and severity. Many of them are relatively mild and do not need surgical intervention, some are fairly easy to deal with, while a proportion are serious and necessitate complex surgery.

Because of the high incidence of congenital cardiac defects most paediatric departments have screening programs for newborn children with Down syndrome. The use of *ultrasound* in screening programs has made the detection of cardiac abnormalities easier and has had the effect of allowing earlier and more effective treatment.

In the authors' recent survey of 46 teenagers in the UK, 19 (41%) had cardiac defects, for which 13 had had surgery in infancy or preschool years.

The diagnosis and treatment of cardiac disorders is highly specialised and is the province of the paediatric cardiologist and paediatric cardiac surgeon.

Detailed information on the different types of cardiac disorders and their treatment as well as support is available from the Down's Heart Group (see page 51). They provide continuing support for teenagers and young adults, not just for children.

There are a small group of teenagers who have severe cardiac abnormalities that could not be surgically repaired when they were babies or young children. These young people may begin to experience increased difficulties in energy and mobility in their teenage years, and they will have reduced life expectancy.

Atlanto-axial instability

Many parents and carers are advised not to allow teenagers with Down syndrome to engage in certain sports such as trampolining and forward rolling. This advice is based on the view that people with Down syndrome are more likely to have difficulties in the top part of the spinal column.

An overview of the development of teenagers with Down syndrome

Some understanding of the anatomy of the area may help to clarify some of the issues (see Figures 12 and 13).

The first vertebra of the spinal column is called the 'atlas' or C1 (1st cervical vertebra). It is a roughly circular bone with two areas on its upper surface which support the skull and the atlas, in turn, rests upon the second neck vertebra which is called the 'axis' or C2 (second cervical vertebra).

The axis has a projection, called the 'odontoid process', which projects upwards inside the circle of the atlas. This bony ring, therefore, contains, among other things, the odontoid process and the upper part of the spinal cord behind it.

If the anatomy of this area is altered so that the odontoid process is pushed backward it could then press upon the spinal cord and damage it.

This occurrence is very rare in people with Down syndrome and the mechanisms are still not properly understood but, at present, some organisations such as the Special Olympic Committee require that people with Down syndrome have been tested for evidence of 'atlanto-axial instability' (a-a instability) as a condition for being accepted for the Special Olympics.

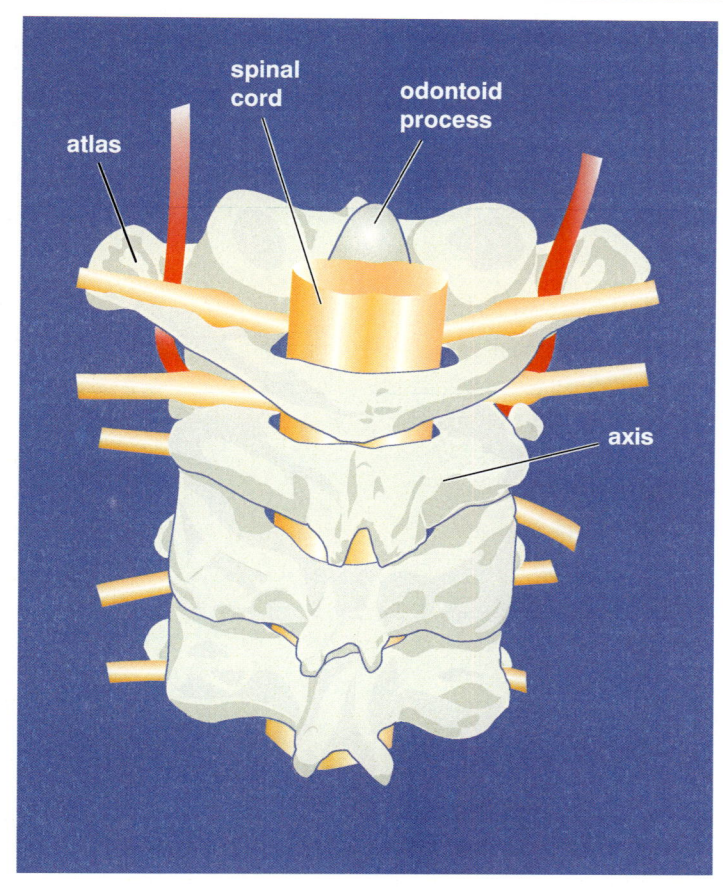

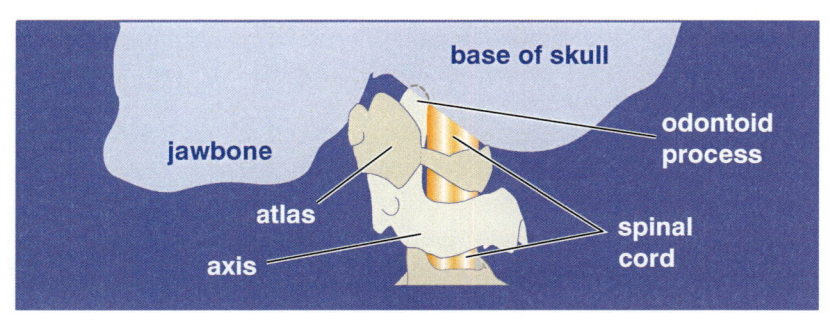

Figure 12. Front view of cervical vertebrae 1 and 2, the odontoid process and the spinal cord (diagram - not to scale)

The test for 'a-a instability' consists of taking x-rays of the neck in several different positions and measuring the distances between various parts of the vertebrae and the spinal cord.

In 1986 the Department of Health of the United Kingdom recommended that people with Down syndrome should have their necks x-rayed before engaging in vigorous sporting activity.

However it later became evident that x-ray examination for 'a-a instability' was not a reliable way of predicting whether there was an increased likelihood of spinal damage in those people who were diagnosed as having 'a-a instability' and the original recommendations of the Department of Health that these x-rays should be carried out were withdrawn in 1995.

'Atlanto-axial instability' remains a controversial issue and although damage to the spinal cord is rare, it is important to point out that when such damage does occur it seldom does so without warning.

The signs of upper spinal cord compression usually start with weakness, new difficulties in walking, not lifting the feet properly and unsteadiness. Pain or

Figure 13. Side view of cervical vertebrae 1 and 2, the odontoid process and the spinal cord (diagram - not to scale)

discomfort in the neck may occur and sometimes the neck may be held in unusual positions.

Bladder and bowel function may be affected and problems with hand and arm function may be later signs.

When possible warning signs do appear it is essential that competent medical intervention is sought as soon as possible in order to establish a diagnosis and institute appropriate treatment.

It is sometimes suggested that a supportive neck collar be worn, especially by people with Down syndrome, if they have pain or discomfort in the neck. This may do more harm than good because supporting the head in this way relieves the neck muscles of the normal exercise they continually perform with the result that they become weak.

Virtually all joints need properly functioning musculature to ensure that they function well and it is, therefore, important that all muscles should maintain their tone and strength with adequate exercise.

The view of many Down syndrome medical advice groups is that there is no good evidence that any form of exercise carries an *additional* risk for people with Down syndrome. In the author's recent survey only 1 of 46 teenagers was reported to have 'slight' atlanto-axial instability, presumably on the basis of an X-ray result, but no symptoms were reported.

Sleep Related Breathing Problems

Difficulties in breathing during the hours of sleep are now known to be relatively common in the population as a whole and one of the commonest and most important of these is Sleep Apnoea - SA. This phrase is used to denote the situation where the passage of air in and out of the lungs is interfered with during sleep.

There are, conventionally, two forms of SA.

The commonest is obstructive sleep apnoea - OSA, which accounts for about 90% of all forms of SA. In this condition the airflow is decreased by factors which produce obstruction of varying degrees in the upper air passages. This may be caused by enlarged tonsils and/or adenoids, small size or other abnormalities of the soft tissues of the airways, infections of these tissues which may cause further narrowing, and several other factors.

Airways obstruction may lead to the level of oxygen in the blood falling and the level of carbon dioxide rising. These, and other factors lead to sleep being disturbed and partial or complete awakening, a change of position and a few deep breaths. The person usually goes back to sleep again until another apnoeic event disturbs them again. These arousal episodes may happen many times during the night and are best understood as protective strategies which have the effect of re-establishing effective air flow. OSA may be associated with strange sleep positions, snoring and restlessness as well as apnoeic episodes.

A less common form of sleep apnoea is central sleep apnoea - CPA, which comprises about 10% of the sleep apnoeas. In this condition the breathing difficulties are related to disordered movement of the diaphragm which is presumed to be caused by disturbances in the centres in the brain which control diaphragmatic movement.

SA is associated with a surprisingly diverse, and often quite serious, number of conditions. Some of the commoner ones are high blood pressure, restricted growth, lung infections and number of daytime behaviour problems such as overactivity, sleepiness and poor attention, thus illustrating the adage that "If you have a bad night you will not have a good day".

The incidence of SA is reported to be 10% of the population over 65 years of age and between 2 to 4% of the middle-aged population of the USA. These figures suggest that sleep disorders are an important problem and there is convincing evidence that the figures are considerably higher in people with Down syndrome. In a UK survey[35] of 91 children with Down syndrome aged from 4 to 19 years, 12% were reported to have apnoeic episodes and this incidence did not change significantly across the age range. Other features thought to be related to sleep apnoea were reported to be very frequent, with loud snoring reported for 43%, sleeping with neck extended for 30%, gagging and choking during sleep for 7%, restlessness for 60% and mouth breathing for 73% of the children with Down syndrome. The incidence of all these difficulties was significantly higher than those reported for the siblings of the children with Down syndrome, a typically developing group of children and a group with learning difficulties but not Down syndrome. The comparison groups were all of a similar age distribution to the group with Down syndrome. This study also found that the presence and severity of sleep disturbance was associated with levels of daytime behaviour difficulties and levels of maternal stress.

If there is good evidence that SA might be present and especially if there are apparently associated difficulties such as undesirable behaviours and/or physical symptoms, the diagnosis should be elucidated in a sleep laboratory where a large number of measurements are taken during an overnight sleep stay.

Once the diagnosis is confirmed a treatment strategy will be worked out so that restful, non-fragmented sleep can be re-established.

Obesity, healthy eating and exercise

The risk of becoming overweight seems to increase for young people with Down syndrome after puberty. For example, an Italian study of 160 children[36] reported that only 14% of those who had not yet reached puberty were overweight, but 66% of those who had reached puberty were overweight based on BMI - Body Mass Index. Body Mass Index is based on the relationship between the individual's height and weight.

In the authors' recent survey of 46 teenagers, 22 (48%) were considered by their parents to be overweight and most of their parents were worried about their son/daughter's weight gain and would have liked advice on how to reduce their weight. This means that parents of teenagers need to particularly aware of encouraging healthy eating and sufficient exercise for their sons and daughters. A balanced diet containing a proper mix of the four key food groups (meat and fish, vegetables and fruit, bread and grains, and dairy products) needs to be encouraged while limiting the intake of foods high in fats and sugars. This is not easy given the kinds of foods encouraged in fast-food outlets and even school canteens.

Useful practical advice on how to encourage healthy eating written by Joan Medlen, a dietician who is also the parent of child with Down syndrome, is available[37] and can be found on the Disability Solutions website (page 54).

Dental care

There are a number of dental abnormalities which are associated with Down syndrome, including late appearance of teeth, missing teeth, some abnormally shaped teeth, abnormal bite as the upper an lower teeth are not normally aligned and an increased risk of gum disease.[38] On the positive side, children with Down syndrome seem to have a significantly lower incidence of dental caries. One study reported that 43% of children with Down syndrome were completely free from tooth decay.

Delayed appearance of teeth affects 75% of children. Sometimes first primary teeth do not appear until 2 years of age, they are not complete before 4 to 5 years and may be retained until 14 to 15 years. This means that many teenagers will still be getting their secondary teeth. Some 43% of teenagers will not get the usual number of teeth and it is at this time that treatment may be required to ensure that teeth are aligned and bite corrected if possible.

All teenagers should have regular dental checks and receive appropriate treatment for dental problems and abnormalities. The incidence of gum disease is reported to be higher in adolescents with Down syndrome than in other adolescents. Gum disease is affected by oral hygiene, dietary control and regular dental visits. Teenagers should be encouraged to brush their teeth after each meal, or at least twice a day. Some authors recommend flossing once a day but this may be difficult for teenagers to manage. The advice on a healthy diet is to avoid sugary, sticky foods.

Puberty and sexual health

Teenagers with Down syndrome experience the same physical and emotional changes during adolescence as other teenagers. Two studies in the UK[3,39] have found that girls with Down syndrome may begin to menstruate about a year earlier on average but this has not been reported in American studies.[40]

The majority of teenagers with Down syndrome cope well with the changes. Most girls learn to take care of their own hygiene needs effectively during their periods. Most boys learn to masturbate only in private.

Research into fertility, sexuality and pregnancy in individuals with Down syndrome is limited. It seems that both girls and boys are fertile though fertility may be lower than is typical in the general population. However, contraception should be considered if young people are sexually active - it should not be assumed that young people with Down syndrome are not fertile. There are recorded cases of men and women with Down syndrome becoming parents.[41,42]

The sexual and emotional needs of teenagers and young people with Down syndrome are the same as those of the rest of the population. Some young people appear to be more sexually aware and active than others, and this is also true of the rest of the population. The opportunity for teenagers with Down syndrome to have a boyfriend or girlfriend and to establish a meaningful relationship may be reduced as their social lives are usually still controlled by their parents and restricted by their limited independent travel skills.

However, increasing numbers of teenagers and adults are forming close relationships, with some establishing permanent partnerships or getting married.

It is important that all young people with Down syndrome learn as much as possible about the ways in which their body is changing and about taking care of their personal hygiene. It is also important that they have good and accurate sex education, which includes all the basic biological facts and includes discussion of relationships, how sexual relationships develop and how people love and care for each other. This is not only important in order to ensure that young people with Down syndrome can enjoy happy and fulfilling relationships, but also to ensure that they are able to protect themselves from advances that they do not want or that are abusive.

Sex education can take place in small steps over a number of years, in a way that is judged to be appropriate for each individual, especially as the personalities and abilities of individuals with Down syndrome varies so widely. Teenagers with Down syndrome should receive the same health care as other teenagers, as appropriate for their sexual development and experience.

All teenagers should have some understanding of intercourse and conception. If likely to be sexually active, then information on contraception and venereal diseases may be appropriate. In the authors' experience, promiscuity in teenage years is unusual, though a wish for a steady relationship is common. Since most teenagers do not wander about the community alone, risks of abuse and concealed sexual relationships are not great. More detailed sex education can usually be provided as relationships are beginning to blossom.

In the authors' experience, most teenagers and adults understand more about sexual development, sexual activity and pregnancy than their parents and others would expect. Most teenagers and adults are also able to act in a mature and responsible way in their relationships, and understand the need for contraception.

Mental Health and Behaviour Problems

Mental disorders

Most people are aware of the physical and social changes which take place during adolescence. However, the nature of the behavioural, perceptual and emotional changes are still not very well understood. There is also some difficulty in distinguishing between more-or-less normal adjustment problems and more serious forms of mental illness.

It is difficult to obtain reliable information on the overall prevalence of mental disorders in Down syndrome because of the poor reliability of diagnosis and the difficulties in obtaining sufficiently large and representative populations of people with Down syndrome.

However, most of the published studies on people with mental disorders and Down syndrome report that virtually all the mental disorders that are found in the population as a whole may occur in people with Down syndrome and it also seems likely that the prevalence of the more serious disorders is lower than in control groups consisting of people with learning disabilities of various types.[43,44]

An overview of the development of teenagers with Down syndrome

It may be that some disorders such as clinical depression, autistic spectrum disorders and attention deficit hyperactivity disorder are more common in people with Down syndrome but evidence for this is not very good at present. Nevertheless is important to be aware that mental disorders may occur in people with Down syndrome and that they need to be treated in the same way as in anyone else.

There may be difficulties in diagnosis where, for example, the person concerned is unable to communicate effectively or manifests the disorder in an unusual way, but it should be possible to obtain a good diagnosis and formulation with the aid of a suitable expert.

Depression

The diagnostic category that causes considerable difficulty at present is covered by the phrase 'depression'. It does seem that clinical depression and serious unhappiness are often confused with each other, and since the management of these two conditions can sometimes be very different it is important to remember that the observation that someone is feeling miserable is only the beginning of the diagnostic process and not the diagnosis itself.

It is probable that a significant number of late adolescents with Down syndrome become chronically miserable and more-or-less withdrawn because they find that many of their childhood expectations have not been realised.

The story of Katrina [not her real name] is an example.

Katrina was told that she had Down syndrome when she was about ten years of age but this was not brought up subsequently. She had two older siblings who included her in most of their leisure activities and the family always went on their, frequent, holidays together. These arrangements stopped fairly abruptly when her siblings become occupied with examinations and boy friends and Katrina found herself both friendless and confronted with the realisation that she could no longer follow in the footsteps of her siblings. She became miserable, withdrawn and consumed with feelings of inadequacy and hopelessness. It took a great deal of help and time before she began to engage with life once more.

Katrina's story is an example of a severe adjustment reaction and not of a severe mental illness.

The presentation of clinical depression is essentially the same in Down syndrome as in any control group.

Self talk

A large percentage of people with Down syndrome of all ages tend to talk to themselves and/or have imaginary friends and this is sometimes a cause concern in their parents and carers. In virtually all cases this perfectly normal and has nothing to do with the hallucinations found in serious mental illnesses.[3,4]

Almost all typically developing children go though a stage of 'self talk' and this is progressively internalised with age. A fair number continue this practice throughout their lives regardless of their level of intelligence.

It is now generally accepted that self talk is merely a form of thinking aloud and serves an adaptive function by helping to think about the various tasks and problems of daily life.

Treatment

None of the above considerations affect the treatment of any person with Down syndrome who has been diagnosed as having a mental disorder since the management of theses disorders in people with Down syndrome should be the best conventional treatment available.

However, because the diagnosis if mental illnesses can some times be difficult and because the likelihood of more than one diagnosis being present at the same time is fairly high it is important exclude conditions such as thyroid diseases, problems with hearing and vision and sleep apnoea..

Behaviour problems

Behaviour problems, autism and ADHD are sometimes considered as mental health issues. These are discussed in the first section of this module on page 25.

Monitoring developmental progress

A number of Down syndrome medical interest groups as well as other organisations provide information and record charts which are particularly helpful in monitoring the health of children with Down syndrome.

These include charts illustrating the changes in height and weight with age to 18 years, developmental milestones and record charts for health checks and their results. These charts help to ensure that health checks are carried out at the appropriate times. These pages are meant to be added to the existing records in the child's Personal Child Health Record Book (PCHR).

In the UK these can be obtained from: Down's Syndrome Medical Interest Group, Children's Centre, City Hospital Campus, Hucknall Road, Nottingham, NG5 1PB. Email: info@dsmig.org.uk http://www.dsmig.org.uk

Excellent information, and videos on heart defects, can be obtained from: Down's Heart Group, 17 Cantilupe Close, Eaton Bray, Dunstable, Bedfordshire, LU6 2EA. Email: Downs_Heart_Group@msn.com http://www.downs-heart.downsnet.org/

UK Guidelines for Paediatricians can be obtained from: Marder, E. and Dennis, J. (1997). Medical management of children with Down's syndrome. *Current Paediatrics*, 7, 1-7.

USA Healthcare Guidelines for Individuals with Down Syndrome, edited by William I. Cohen, can be found in: *Down Syndrome: A Promising Future Together*, eds. Hassold, T. J. and Patterson, D. (1998). Wiley-Liss, with a 1999 Revision in *Down Syndrome Quarterly*, 4 (3), 1-16, available at: http://www.denison.edu/dsq/health99.shtml

The most informative website providing information on health and medical issues is that provided by Len Leshin, a paediatrician and father of a child with Down syndrome, at: http://www.ds-health.com/

A detailed *Down Syndrome Issues and Information* series of Health modules to inform doctors and healthcare professionals as well as parents, will be available during 2002.

Useful website resources on healthy eating, autism, ADHD, behaviour and sexuality at www.disabilitysolutions.org

References

1. Buckley, S.J., Bird, G., Sacks, B. and Archer, T. (in press). The development of teenagers with Down syndrome in 1987 and 1999: implications for families and schools. *Down Syndrome News and Update*, 2.
2. Buckley, S.J., Bird, G., Sacks, B., and Archer, T. (in press). A comparison of mainstream and special school education for teenagers with Down syndrome: effects on social and academic development. *Down Syndrome Research and Practice*, 8.
3. Buckley, S. and Sacks, B. (1987) *The adolescent with Down syndrome: Life for the teenager and for the family.* Portsmouth, UK: Portsmouth Polytechnic.
4. McGuire, D.E. and Chicoine, B.A. (1999). Life issues of adolescence and adults with Down syndrome. In T.J. Hassold and D. Patterson, (Eds.) *Down Syndrome: A promising future together.* New York, USA: Wiley-Liss. pp. 205-220.
5. *Listen to us: The Down syndrome women's guide for a healthy life.* Video. The Down Syndrome Association of NSW Inc. PO Box 2356, North Parramatta, 1750 Australia. See at www.hartingale.com.au/~dsansw/
6. The Down to Earth Group video and worksheets. Down's Syndrome Association. 155, Mitcham Road, London, SW17 9PG. See at www.downs-syndrome.org.uk.
7. Farrell, M. (1996). Continuing literacy development. In B. Stratford and P. Gunn, (Eds.) *New Approaches to Down syndrome.* London, UK: Cassell. pp. 280-299.
8. Fowler, A., Doherty, B.J. and Boynton, L. (1995). Basis of reading skill in young adults with Down syndrome. In L. Nadel and D. Rosenthal, (Eds.) *Down syndrome: Living and Learning in the community.* New York, USA: Wiley-Liss. pp. 182-196.
9. Sparrow, S.S., Balla, D.A. and Cicchetti, D.V. (1984). Vineland Adaptive Behaviour Scale. Minnesota, USA: American Guidance Service.
10. Conners, C.K. (1997). *Conners Rating Scales-Revised.* Toronto, Canada: Multi-Health Systems Inc.
11. Chapman, R.S. (1997). Language development. In S.M. Pueschel and M. Sustrova, (Eds.) *Adolescents with Down syndrome: towards a more fulfilling life.* Baltimore,USA: Paul H. Brookes Publishing. pp. 99-110.
12. Gunn, P. and Crombie, M. (1996). Language and speech. In B. Stratford and P. Gunn, (Eds.) *New Approaches to Down syndrome.* London, UK: Cassell. pp. 249-267.
13. Fowler, A. (1999). The challenge of linguistic mastery. In T.J. Hassold and D. Patterson, (Eds.) (1999) *Down Syndrome: A promising future together.* New York, USA: Wiley-Liss. pp. 165-184.
14. Chapman, R.S. (2001). Language, cognition, and short-term memory in individuals with Down syndrome. *Down Syndrome Research and Practice*, 7 (1), 1-7.
15. Cuskelly, M. and Gunn, P. (1997). Behaviour concerns. In Pueschel, S.M. and Sustrova, M. (Eds.) *Adolescents with Down syndrome: towards a more fulfilling life.* Baltimore, USA: Paul H. Brookes Publishing. pp 111-128.
16. Stores, R., Stores, G., Fellows, B. and Buckley, S. (1998). Daytime behaviour problems and maternal stress in children with Down syndrome, their siblings, and non-intellectually disabled and other intellectually disabled peers. *Journal of Intellectual Disability Research*. 42 (3) 228-237.
17. Cuskelly, M. and Gunn, P. (1991). Behaviour problems in adolescents with Down syndrome. In C.D. Denholm, (Ed.) *Adolescents with Down syndrome: International perspectives on research and development.* Victoria, Canada: University of Victoria. pp. 53-62.

18. Stores, R., Stores, G., Fellows, B. and Buckley, S. (1998). A factor analysis of sleep problems and their psychological associations in children with Down syndrome. *Journal of Applied Research in Intellectual Disabilities.* 11 (4) 345-354.
19. Turner, P. and Sloper, P. (1996). Behaviour problems among children with Down's syndrome; Prevalence, persistence and parental appraisal. *Journal of Applied Research in Intellectual Disabilities.* 9 (2) 129-144.
20. Cunningham, C.C. (1996). Families with children with Down syndrome. *Down Syndrome Research and Practice.* 4 (3) 87-95.
21. Bochner, S. and Pieterse, M. (1996). Teenagers with Down syndrome in a time of changing policies and practices: Report on a study of the progress of New South Wales teenagers who were born between 1971 and 1978. *International Journal of Disability, Development and Education*, 43 (1), 75-95.
22. Rynders, J., Abery, B.H., Spiker, D., Olive, M.L., Sheran, C.P. and Zajac, R.J. (1997). Improving educational programming for individuals with Down syndrome: Engaging the fuller competence. *Down Syndrome Quarterly*, 2 (1), 1-11.
23. Freeman, S.F.N. and Hodapp, R.M. (2000). Educating children with Down syndrome: linking behavioral characteristics to promising intervention strategies. *Down Syndrome Quarterly*, 5 (1), 1-9.
24. Chapman, R.S. and Hesketh, L.J. (2000). Behavioural phenotype of individuals with Down syndrome. *Mental Retardation and Developmental Disability Research Reviews*, 6, 84-95.
25. Laws, G., Buckley, S.J., Bird, G., MacDonald, J., and Broadley, I. (1995). The influence of reading instruction on language and memory development in children with Down syndrome. *Down Syndrome Research and Practice*, 3 (2), 59-64.
26. Laws, G., MacDonald, J., Buckley, S.J., and Broadley, I. (1995). Long-term maintenance of memory skills taught to children with Down syndrome. *Down Syndrome Research and Practice*, 3 (3), 103-109.
27. Numicon 'At home' and Numicon Nursery Kit published by Numicon Ltd., available from The Down Syndrome Educational Trust.
28. Cunningham, C.C., Glenn, S., Lorenz, S., Cuckle, P. and Shepperdson, B. (1998). Trends in outcomes in educational placements for children with Down syndrome. *European Journal of Special Needs Education*, 13, 225-237.
29. Laws, G., Byrne, A. and Buckley, S. (2000). Language and memory development in children with Down syndrome at mainstream and special schools: a comparison. *Educational Psychology*, 20 (4) 447-457.
30. Van Riper, M. (1999). Living with Down syndrome: the family experience. *Down Syndrome Quarterly*, 4, 1-11.
31. Krauss, M.W. and Seltzer, M.M. (1995). Long-term caring: family experiences over the life course. In L. Nadel and D. Rosenthal (Eds.) *Down syndrome: Living and Learning in the community.* New York, USA: Wiley-Liss.
32. Shott, S.R. (2000). Down Syndrome: Common Pediatric Ear, Nose and Throat Problems. *Down Syndrome Quarterly*, 5 (2), 1-6.
33. McNeill, B. (1991). Hearing loss in adolescents with Down syndrome. In C.D. Denholm, (Ed.) *Adolescents with Down syndrome: International perspectives on research and development.* Victoria, Canada: University of Victoria.
34. Marcell, M.M. (1995). Relationships between hearing and auditory cognition in Down's syndrome youth. *Down Syndrome Research and Practice*, 3 (3), 75-79.
35. Stores, R., Stores, G. and Buckley, S. (1996). The pattern of sleep problems in children with Down's syndrome and other intellectual disabilities. *Journal of Applied Research in Intellectual Disabilities*, 9 (2) 145-158.
36. Crino, A., Ciampalini, P., Digilio, M.C., Giannotti, A. *et al.* (1996). Growth pattern and pubertal development in Down syndrome: A longitudinal and cross-sectional study. *Developmental Brain Dysfunction*, 9 (2-3) 72-79.

37. Medlen, J.E. (1999). Weight management in Down syndrome - the school and adolescent years. Disability Solutions: see website at www.disabilitysolutions.org and reprinted in *Down Syndrome News and Update* 1999. 1 (4) 185-188.
38. Chiang, T. (1991) the dental needs of adolescents with Down syndrome. In C.D. Denholm, (Ed.) *Adolescents with Down syndrome: International perspectives on research and development.* Victoria, Canada: University of Victoria. pp. 129-136.
39. Evans, A.L. and McKinlay, I.A. (1988) Sexual maturation in girls with severe mental handicap. *Child: Care, Health and Development.* 14 (1) 59-69.
40. Pueschel, S.M. (1997) Adolescent development and sexual maturation. In S.M. Pueschel and M. Sustrova, (Eds.) *Adolescents with Down syndrome: towards a more fulfilling life.* Baltimore, USA: Paul H. Brookes Publishing. pp. 35-38.
41. Edwards, J. (1988). Sexuality, marriage and parenting for persons with Down syndrome. In S.M. Pueschel (Ed.) *The young person with Down syndrome: transition from adolescence to adulthood.* Baltimore, USA: Paul H. Brookes Publishing. pp. 187-204.
42. Brown, R.I. (1995). Social life, dating and marriage. In L. Nadel and D. Rosenthal, (Eds.) *Down syndrome: Living and Learning in the community.* New York, USA: Wiley-Liss. pp. 43-49.
43. Harris, J.C. (1988). Psychological adaptation and psychiatric disorders in adolescents and young adults with Down syndrome. In S.M. Pueschel (Ed.) *The young person with Down syndrome: transition from adolescence to adulthood.* Baltimore, USA: Paul H. Brookes Publishing. pp. 35-52.
44. Myers, B.A. (1997). Psychiatric disorders. In S.M. Pueschel and M. Sustrova, (Eds.) *Adolescents with Down syndrome: towards a more fulfilling life.* Baltimore, USA: Paul H. Brookes Publishing. pp. 129-144.
45. Powers, L.E. and Sikora, D.M. (1997). Promoting adolescent self-competence. In S.M. Pueschel and M. Sustrova, (Eds.) *Adolescents with Down syndrome: towards a more fulfilling life.* Baltimore, USA: Paul H. Brookes Publishing. pp. 71-90.
46. Heyne, L.A., Schlein, S.J. and Rynders, J.E. (1997). Promoting quality of life through recreational participation. In S.M. Pueschel and M. Sustrova, (Eds.) *Adolescents with Down syndrome: towards a more fulfilling life.* Baltimore, USA: Paul H. Brookes Publishing. pp. 317-340.
47. Rynders J. and Low, M.L. (2001). "Adrift" in the mainstream: The need to structure communicative interactions between students with Down syndrome and their non-disabled peers. *Down Syndrome Quarterly*, 6 (1) 1-8.
48. Quail, S. (2000). *The social inclusion of pupils with Down syndrome in mainstream secondary schools.* Unpublished B.Sc. dissertation. University of Portsmouth.
49. Workshop dates and details in The Down Syndrome Educational Trust's Services Catalogue 2001/2.

Useful book resources

Pueschel, S.M. and Sustrova, M. (Eds.) (1997). *Adolescents with Down syndrome: towards a more fulfilling life.* Baltimore,USA: Paul H. Brookes Publishing.

Nadel, L. and Rosenthal, D. (Eds.) (1995). *Down syndrome: Living and Learning in the community.* New York, USA: Wiley-Liss.

Hassold, T.J. and Patterson, D. (Eds.) (1999). *Down Syndrome: A promising future together.* New York, USA: Wiley-Liss.

Website resources

Useful website resources on healthy eating, autism, ADHD, behaviour and sexuality at www.disabilitysolutions.org